Language Arts Handbook
Grade Two
Table of Contents

This book is designed to help review and reinforce the language skills that students will master in the second grade. It is a comprehensive handbook that addresses a broad range of the language concepts that students will encounter at this grade level. It can be used effectively as a tool to reinforce language skills at school or at home, or to keep skills sharp over extended vacations.

Organization

These activities are designed to reinforce the language skills that are important for students in the second grade. This book is divided into eight units: Reading and Spelling, Grammar, Sentences, Vocabulary and Usage, Capitalization and Punctuation, Kinds of Writing, Paragraphs, and Book Skills and Comprehension. Each section focuses on one or two related concepts, and review pages appear at the beginning of each unit to give teachers or parents the opportunity to gauge understanding and to signal if more practice is needed.

- **Reading and Spelling.** An important part of language skills study for students in the second grade is strengthening their grasp of the relationships between letters and sounds. Here students work with beginning sounds, ending sounds, and vowel sounds.

- **Grammar.** Several major parts of speech—nouns, verbs, adjectives, pronouns, compound words, and contractions—are defined, and students are given the opportunity for practice.

- **Sentences.** Students learn the parts of a sentence, the different kinds of sentences, how to join sentences, and how to write clear, descriptive sentences.

- **Vocabulary and Usage.** Students review prepositions, synonyms, antonyms, prefixes, and suffixes, and study common spelling problems.

- **Capitalization and Punctuation.** Students study the common uses of capitalization, such as the beginning of sentences, names of people and places, the word *I*, days, months, and titles. Students practice correct usage of the period, the question mark, the exclamation point, and the apostrophe.

- **Kinds of Writing.** Several common types of writing are reviewed, including story, rhyme, poem, friendly letter, invitation, thank-you note, envelope addressing, journal entry, and book report.

- **Paragraphs.** Paragraphs are defined, and good paragraph writing is explained. Students examine the different types of paragraphs, including how-to, comparing, contrasting, explaining, defining, describing and persuading — and practice writing each type.

- **Book Skills and Comprehension.** Students review the parts of a book and dictionary skills. Fiction and nonfiction writing is addressed. Important reading comprehension skills are reviewed, such as drawing conclusions, cause and effect, identifying details, and predicting outcomes, among others.

Use

This book is designed for independent use by students who have been introduced to the skills and concepts described. Copies of the activities can be given to individuals, pairs of students, or small groups for completion. They may be used as a center activity. If students are familiar with the content, the worksheets may also be used as homework.

To begin, determine the implementation that fits your students' needs and your classroom structure. The following plan suggests a format for this implementation.

1. **Explain** the purpose of the worksheets to your students. Let them know that these activities will be fun as well as helpful.

2. **Review** the mechanics of how you want the students to work with the activities. Do you want them to work in groups? Are the activities for homework?

3. **Decide** how you would like to use the assessments. They can be given before and after a unit to determine progress, or just after a unit to assess how well the concepts are learned. Determine whether you will send the tests home or keep them in the students' portfolios.

4. **Introduce** students to the process and the purpose of the activities. Go over the directions. Work with children when they have difficulty. Work only a few pages at a time to avoid pressure.

5. **Do** a practice activity together.

Additional Notes

- **Parent Communication.** Send the Letter to Parents home with students so that parents will know what to expect and how they can best help their child.

- **Bulletin Board.** Display completed work to show student progress.

- **Assessments.** The first page of each unit is a unit assessment. Unit One has three assessments that can be administered as students complete each section of the unit. Unit Eight has two assessments. You can use the tests as diagnostic tools by administering them before children begin the activities. After children have completed each unit, let them retake the unit test(s) to see the progress they have made. The assessments may be sent home or kept in portfolios for parent/teacher conferencing.

- **Center Activities.** Use the worksheets as a center activity to give students the opportunity to work cooperatively.

- **Have fun.** Working with these activities can be fun as well as meaningful for you and your students.

Dear Parent,

During this school year, our class will be using an activity book to reinforce the language skills that we are learning. By working together, we can be sure that your child not only masters these language skills but also becomes confident in his or her abilities.

From time to time, I may send home activity sheets. To help your child, please consider the following suggestions:

- Provide a quiet place to work.
- Go over the directions together.
- Encourage your child to do his or her best.
- Check the lesson when it is complete.
- Note improvements as well as problems.

Help your child maintain a positive attitude about the activities. Let your child know that each lesson provides an opportunity to have fun and to learn. Above all, enjoy this time you spend with your child. As your child's language skills develop, he or she will feel your support.

Thank you for your help.

Cordially,

Name _____ Date _____

Unit One Assessment: Beginning Sounds

✏️ Read the three words in each row. Circle the two words that have the same beginning sound.

1. king   cup   hall
2. kite   home   who
3. scene   ceiling   call
4. jar   gym   gas
5. come   kick   hand
6. nice   mouse   gnat
7. write   rice   neat
8. knock   king   nice

✏️ Choose the correct pair or group of beginning letters from the box to complete each word. Use each pair or group only once.

br, cr, tr, fr, gr

9. _____ ue
10. _____ og
11. _____ ayon
12. _____ een
13. _____ other

spl, str, spr, shr, thr

19. _____ it
20. _____ ing
21. _____ unk
22. _____ ong
23. _____ oat

sp, sk, st, sm, sn

14. _____ eck
15. _____ ap
16. _____ ell
17. _____ irt
18. _____ ay

tw, ch, th, sh, ph

24. _____ unk
25. _____ ice
26. _____ one
27. _____ eep
28. _____ em

Name _____   Date _____

Unit One Assessment: Ending Sounds

✏️ Read the three words in each row. Circle the two words that have the same ending sound.

1. shell   doll   cuff
2. cliff   mill   muff
3. page   whiz   bridge
4. voice   class   clock
5. is   shook   fuzz
6. black   look   spoons
7. glass   rice   has
8. pass   cottage   village

✏️ Choose the correct pair or group of beginning letters from the box to complete each word. Use each pair or group only once.

st, nd, ld, nt, sk

9. fir _____
10. squi _____
11. wor _____
12. rou _____
13. ta _____

nk, ng, ph, gh, st

19. spri _____
20. bur _____
21. dri _____
22. lau _____
23. gra _____

ft, sp, sh, ch, th

14. ea _____
15. bru _____
16. gra _____
17. gi _____
18. tee _____

nd, sh, ft, sk, ng

24. sou _____
25. de _____
26. di _____
27. fli _____
28. so _____

Name _____   Date _____

Unit One Assessment: Vowel Sounds

✏ Read the three words in each row. Circle the two words that have the same vowel sound.

1. would   were   good
2. base   snail   snow
3. play   time   tail
4. key   ship   leaf
5. pity   field   cone
6. see   me   turn
7. ride   sell   bright
8. kind   sky   down
9. flow   pie   high
10. fall   open   goat
11. blow   road   send
12. rope   cane   old
13. use   fuse   find
14. dune   done   tube
15. two   night   boot
16. chew   soup   teeth
17. horn   cube   warm
18. tame   door   more
19. heard   fly   serve
20. gone   girl   word
21. turn   grow   her
22. farm   yarn   wind
23. fume   care   chair
24. bear   deer   hair
25. cheer   dear   fair

Name _____ Date _____

Beginning Sounds: Consonants

☞ Every letter is a **consonant** except <u>a</u>, <u>e</u>, <u>i</u>, <u>o</u>, <u>u</u>, and sometimes <u>y</u>. The first letter in each of these words is a consonant. Each consonant stands for a beginning sound.

<u>t</u> as in <u>toad</u>   <u>g</u> as in <u>garden</u>

<u>p</u> as in <u>put</u>   <u>m</u> as in <u>music</u>

 Practice

Say the name for each picture. Listen to each beginning sound. Write words from the box that begin with the same sound under each picture. Write words with the same beginning sound under each other.

gone	tell	man	gold
my	pin	too	poor

1.

_____

_____

3.

_____

_____

2.

_____

_____

4.

_____

_____

Language Arts 2, SV 3888-3

Name _____ Date _____

Beginning Sounds: Consonants

☞ The first letter in each of these words is a consonant. Each consonant stands for a beginning sound.

w as in **walk**   **y** as in **you**
n as in **near**   **d** as in **day**
b as in **bicycle**   **l** as in **load**
f as in **fast**   **z** as in **zoom**
v as in **very**

✎ **Practice**

Read the words in the box. Listen to each beginning sound.

worm	now	van	week
boat	vase	zoo	yard
fox	duck	young	lion

The words from the box are shown below. Stars are where the beginning consonants should be. Write the words with the right consonant in place of the stars.

1. ★oat _____

2. ★eek _____

3. ★ow _____

4. ★ox _____

5. ★orm _____

6. ★oung _____

7. ★ion _____

8. ★oo _____

9. ★uck _____

10. ★ase _____

11. ★ard _____

12. ★an _____

Name _____ Date _____

Beginning Sounds: /j/, /g/, /s/, /sc/, /c/

☞ The letters j and g stand for the beginning sound you hear in the word jump.

j as in jar   g as in gym

☞ The letters s, c, and sc stand for the beginning sound you hear in the word sand.

s as in saw   c as in ceiling   sc as in scene

☞ **Practice**

Say the name for each picture. Listen to each beginning sound. Write words from the box that begin with the same sound under each picture. Write words with the same beginning sound under each other.

giraffe	joke	scent	job	said	giant
city	sausage	cent	soon	just	gym

1.

_____

_____

_____

_____

_____

2.

_____

_____

_____

_____

_____

Language Arts 2, SV 3888-3

Beginning Sounds: /c/, /k/, /h/, /wh/

☞ The letters <u>c</u> and <u>k</u> stand for the beginning sound you hear in the word <u>cat</u>.

<u>c</u> as in <u>care</u>   <u>k</u> as in <u>kind</u>

☞ The letters <u>h</u> and <u>wh</u> stand for the beginning sound you hear in the word <u>hot</u>.

<u>h</u> as in <u>head</u>   <u>wh</u> as in <u>who</u>

☞ **Practice**

Read the three words in each row. Write the two words that have the same beginning sound.

1. king	cup	hall	_____	_____
2. kite	home	who	_____	_____
3. hat	car	house	_____	_____
4. whole	cow	kitten	_____	_____
5. hill	kite	cave	_____	_____
6. hope	cold	cat	_____	_____
7. carrot	keep	hose	_____	_____
8. happy	kind	hut	_____	_____
9. come	kick	hand	_____	_____
10. hit	can	horse	_____	_____
11. had	key	kind	_____	_____
12. hello	help	color	_____	_____
13. cage	his	cane	_____	_____
14. kite	hold	cut	_____	_____
15. whom	hen	kept	_____	_____

Beginning Sounds: /n/, /kn/, /gn/, /r/, /wr/

☞   The letters <u>n</u>, <u>kn</u>, and <u>gn</u> stand for the beginning sound you hear in the word <u>name</u>.

<u>n</u> as in <u>nice</u>   <u>kn</u> as in <u>knock</u>   <u>gn</u> as in <u>gnat</u>

☞   The letters <u>r</u> and <u>wr</u> stand for the beginning sound you hear in the word <u>rake</u>.

<u>r</u> as in <u>right</u>   <u>wr</u> as in <u>wrong</u>

☞ **Practice**

Say the name for each picture. Listen to each beginning sound. Write words from the box that begin with the same sound under each picture. Write words with the same beginning sound under each other.

ring	knew	none	gnat	wrong	ruler
robin	know	neat	wrap	gnaw	wrote

1.

2.

_____

_____

_____

_____

_____

_____

_____

_____

_____

_____

Beginning Sounds: /br/, /fr/, /cr/, /gr/, /tr/

☞ The first two letters in each word below are consonants. The two letters stand for the beginning sounds you hear in each word.

br as in **break**   **fr** as in **freeze**

cr as in **crawl**   **gr** as in **great**

tr as in **troll**

✎ **Practice**

Read the words in the box. Listen to the beginning sounds.

brother	cream	true	from
green	ground	crack	broken
treat	frog	fresh	crayon

The words from the box are shown below. Two shapes are where the beginning consonants should be. Write the words with the right consonants in place of the shapes.

1. ★❤other _____

2. ●❤een _____

3. ■❤og _____

4. ■❤esh _____

5. ◆❤ack _____

6. ★❤oken _____

7. ★❤ue _____

8. ★❤ound _____

9. ★❤ayon _____

10. ★❤om _____

11. ★❤eam _____

12. ★❤eat _____

Name _____   Date _____

Beginning Sounds: /sp/, /sk/, /st/, /sm/, /sn/

 The first two letters in each word below are consonants. The two letters stand for the beginning sounds you hear in each word.

sp as in **spill**   **sk** as in **skin**

st as in **stair**   **sm** as in **small**

sn as in **snow**

✏️ **Practice**

Read the words in the box. Listen to the beginning sounds.

snake	smart	sky	smell	skip
stay	snap	snout	spoke	sport
step	smoke	stamp	stop	speck

Say the name for each picture. Listen to the beginning sounds. Write words from the box that begin with the same sounds under each picture. Write words with the same beginning sounds under each other.

1.

_____

_____

3.

_____

_____

5.

_____

_____

2.

_____

_____

_____

4.

_____

_____

_____

Beginning Sounds: /spl/, /spr/, /str/, /shr/, /squ/

☞ The first three letters in each word below are consonants. The three letters stand for the beginning sounds you hear in each word.

spl as in **split**   **spr** as in **spread**

str as in **string**   **shr** as in **shrimp**

☞ The letters <u>squ</u> stand for the beginning sounds you hear in <u>square</u>. ☐

✏ **Practice**

Read the words in the box. Listen to the beginning sounds.

spring	spray	squeeze	shrink
street	splinter	shrunk	squirrel
squint	strong	splash	squeak

The words from the box are shown below. Three shapes are where the beginning letters should be. Write the words with the right letters in place of the shapes.

1. ●■★ash _____

2. ●■▲ay _____

3. ●❤◆irrel _____

4. ●◗▲ink_____

5. ●◗■▲eet _____

6. ●❤◆int _____

7. ●❤◆eeze _____

8. ●◗▲unk _____

9. ●■▲ing _____

10. ●❤◆eak _____

11. ●◗■▲ong _____

12. ●■★inter _____

Name _____   Date _____

Beginning Sounds: /tw/, /thr/

☞   The first two letters in the word below are consonants. The two letters stand for the beginning sounds you hear in the word.

tw as in twenty

☞   The first three letters in the word below are consonants. The three letters stand for the beginning sounds you hear in the word.

thr as in three

☞ **Practice**

Say the name for each numeral below. Listen to the beginning sounds. Then write words from the box that begin with the same sounds under each number picture. Write words with the same beginning sounds under each other.

twins	throat	twig	through	thread
throne	twinkle	twice	throw	twelve

1.

_____

_____

_____

_____

2. 3

_____

_____

_____

_____

Unit One: Reading and Spelling

Language Arts 2, SV 3888-3

Name _____   Date _____

Beginning Sounds: /ch/, /sh/, /th/, /ph/

☞ The first two letters in each word below are consonants. The two letters stand for the beginning sounds you hear in each word.

ch as in **chuckle**   **sh** as in **shoe**
th as in **that**   **ph** as in **phone**

 **Practice**

Read the words in the box. Listen to the beginning sounds.

chicken	shark	they	them
phone	the	cheese	ship
then	shirt	phonograph	sheep

The words from the box are shown below. Two shapes are where the beginning consonants should be. Write the words with the right consonants in place of the shapes.

1. ●★ark _____   7. ▲❤em _____

2. ●❤icken _____   8. ★❤ip _____

3. ▲❤en _____   9. ▲❤e _____

4. ●❤eese _____   10. ★❤eep _____

5. ★❤irt _____   11. ◆❤onograph _____

6. ▲❤ey _____   12. ◆❤one _____

Name _____ Date _____

Ending Sounds: /ll/, /ff/

 The last two letters in the words below are consonants. The two letters stand for the ending sound you hear in each word.

ll as in <u>tell</u>   **ff as in <u>off</u>**

✏ Practice

Read the words in the box. Listen to each ending sound.

shell	ball	doll
muff	hill	cuff
mill	cliff	well

Write the word from the box that names each picture.

1.

_____

2.

_____

3.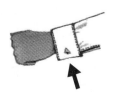

_____

4.

_____

5.

_____

6.

_____

7.

_____

8.

_____

9.

_____

Name _____ Date _____

Ending Sounds: /ss/, /ce/, /s/, /z/, /zz/, /ge/, /dge/, /k/, /ck/

☞ The letters <u>ss</u> and <u>ce</u> stand for the ending sound you hear in the word <u>grass</u>.

<u>ss</u> as in <u>glass</u>   **<u>ce</u> as in <u>place</u>**

☞ The letters <u>s</u>, <u>z</u>, and <u>zz</u> stand for the ending sound you hear in the word <u>was</u>.

<u>s</u> as in <u>trees</u>   **<u>zz</u> as in <u>buzz</u>**   **<u>z</u> as in <u>quiz</u>**

☞ The letters <u>ge</u> and <u>dge</u> stand for the ending sound you hear in the word <u>large</u>.

<u>ge</u> as in <u>change</u>   **<u>dge</u> as in <u>porridge</u>**

☞ The letters <u>k</u> and <u>ck</u> stand for the ending sound you hear in the word <u>look</u>.

<u>k</u> as in <u>cook</u>   **<u>ck</u> as in <u>clock</u>**

☞ **Practice**

Read the three words in each row. Write the two words that have the same ending sound.

1. page	whiz	bridge	_____	_____
2. voice	class	clock	_____	_____
3. is	fuzz	shook	_____	_____
4. place	whiz	has	_____	_____
5. clock	cage	book	_____	_____
6. has	bridge	fuzz	_____	_____
7. cottage	pass	village	_____	_____
8. black	spoons	cook	_____	_____

Ending Sounds: /st/, /nd/, /ld/, /nt/, /sk/, /ft/, /sp/

☞   The last two letters in each word below are consonants. The two letters stand for the ending sounds you hear in each word.

st as in **best**   **nd** as in **hand**   **ld** as in **hold**
nt as in **hunt**   **sk** as in **desk**   **ft** as in **soft**
sp as in **crisp**

☞   **Practice**

Read the words in the box. Listen to the ending sounds.

grasp	test	clasp	past	gift
want	gold	ask	friend	world
lift	squint	around	mask	kind

The words from the box are shown below. Spaces are where the ending consonants should be. Finish the words. Write the correct consonants in the spaces.

1. li ____ ____

2. squi ____ ____

3. wor ____ ____

4. frie ____ ____

5. arou ____ ____

6. cla ____ ____

7. ma ____ ____

8. gi ____ ____

9. gra ____ ____

10. pa ____ ____

11. wa ____ ____

12. ki ____ ____

13. te ____ ____

14. go ____ ____

15. a ____ ____

Unit One: Reading and Spelling

Language Arts 2, SV 3888-3

Ending Sounds: /sh/, /ch/, /th/, /nk/, /ng/, /ph/, /gh/

☞ The last two letters in each word below are consonants. The two letters stand for the ending sound you hear in each word.

sh as in **bush**   **ch** as in **branch**
th as in **with**   **nk** as in **wink**
ng as in **spring**   **ph** as in **graph**
gh as in **enough**

☞ **Practice**

Read the words in the box. Listen to each ending sound.

bank	each	dish	rough	teeth
mouth	thank	brush	such	laugh
photograph	rang	wish	thing	much
drink	skunk	which	hunting	bunk

The words from the box are shown below. Two spaces are where the ending consonants should be. Finish the words. Write the correct consonants in the spaces.

1. ba __ __   6. rou __ __   11. mu __ __   16. di __ __

2. ra __ __   7. mou __ __   12. tee __ __   17. ea __ __

3. thi __ __   8. tha __ __   13. su __ __   18. lau __ __

4. bru __ __   9. photogra __ __   14. sku __ __   19. whi __ __

5. wi __ __   10. bu __ __   15. dri __ __   20. hunti __ __

Language Arts 2, SV 3888-3

Vowel Sounds: Vowels

☞ The letters <u>a</u>, <u>e</u>, <u>i</u>, <u>o</u>, <u>u</u> are vowels.

☞ The letter <u>a</u> stands for the vowel sound you hear in <u>sat</u>.

☞ The letter <u>i</u> stands for the vowel sound you hear in <u>ship</u>.

☞ The letter <u>o</u> stands for the vowel sound you hear in <u>rock</u>.

☞ The letters <u>e</u> and <u>ea</u> stand for the vowel sound you hear in <u>end</u>.

<u>e</u> as in <u>pet</u>   **<u>ea</u> as in <u>head</u>**

☞ The letters <u>u</u> and <u>ou</u> stand for the vowel sound you hear in <u>sun</u>.

<u>u</u> as in <u>jump</u>   **<u>ou</u> as in <u>young</u>**

✏ **Practice**

Say the name for each picture. Listen to each vowel sound. Write words from the box that have the same vowel sound under each picture. Write words with the same vowel sound under each other.

touch	rug	win	plan	red
pot	mop	bread	is	back

1.

_____

_____

3.

_____

_____

5.

_____

_____

2.

_____

_____

4.

_____

_____

Name _____   Date _____

Vowel Sounds: /oo/, /ou/

☞ The letters <u>oo</u> and <u>ou</u> stand for the vowel sound you hear in the word <u>book</u>.

<u>oo</u> as in <u>took</u>   **<u>ou</u> as in <u>should</u>**

✐ **Practice**

Read the words in the box. Listen to each vowel sound.

would	hood	foot	brook	good
look	cook	shook	could	stood

The words from the box are shown below. Spaces are where the letters that stand for vowel sounds should be. Finish the words. Write the correct letters in the spaces.

1. h ____ ____ d

2. w ____ ____ ld

3. c ____ ____ k

4. f ____ ____ t

5. g ____ ____ d

6. c ____ ____ ld

7. st ____ ____ d

8. br ____ ____ k

9. l ____ ____ k

10. sh ____ ____ k

Finish each sentence. Use the words from the box.

11. The water in the_____ is cold.

12. Please put your shoe on your _____.

13. The apple pie tastes so _____.

14. My jacket has a warm _____.

15. Will you _____ dinner tonight?

Name _____   Date _____

Vowel Sounds: /a-e/, /ai/, /ay/

☞ The vowel sound you hear in the word <u>game</u> can be spelled
three ways.

<u>a</u>-consonant-<u>e</u> as in <u>base</u>
<u>ai</u> as in <u>wait</u>
<u>ay</u> as in <u>play</u>

☞ **Practice**

Name the picture.

Listen to the vowel sound.

Read the words in each row. Write the word that has the same
vowel sound that you hear in the picture name.

1. now	name	nose	_____
2. look	line	late	_____
3. why	way	were	_____
4. time	take	tell	_____
5. dance	day	do	_____
6. rain	ran	run	_____
7. sat	same	sun	_____
8. came	come	cone	_____
9. stay	stand	stood	_____
10. like	lake	look	_____
11. date	did	down	_____
12. snail	snow	sniff	_____

Name _____ Date _____

Vowel Sounds: /ee/, /ea/, /y/, /e/, /ey/, /ie/

☞ The vowel sound you hear in the word <u>she</u> can be spelled six ways.

<u>ee</u> as in <u>see</u>   <u>ea</u> as in <u>leaf</u>
<u>y</u> as in <u>pity</u>   <u>e</u> as in <u>me</u>
<u>ey</u> as in <u>donkey</u>   <u>ie</u> as in <u>relief</u>

☞ **Practice**

Name the picture.

Listen to the vowel sound.

Read the words in each row. Write the word that has the same vowel sound that you hear in the picture name.

1. king	key	kick	_____
2. say	seed	sing	_____
3. pea	pin	pat	_____
4. chief	chip	choose	_____
5. care	carry	cat	_____
6. shoe	she	ship	_____
7. we	wet	want	_____
8. field	five	fan	_____
9. teeth	tooth	time	_____
10. happy	have	hill	_____
11. tune	turkey	turn	_____
12. reach	rich	run	_____

Name _____ Date _____

Vowel Sounds: /i-e/, /y/, /igh/, /ie/, /i/

 The vowel sound you hear in the word <u>like</u> can be spelled five ways.

> **<u>i</u>-consonant-<u>e</u> as in <u>ride</u>**   **<u>y</u> as in <u>sky</u>**
> **<u>igh</u> as in <u>light</u>**   **<u>ie</u> as in <u>pie</u>**
> **<u>i</u> as in <u>kind</u>**

✎ **Practice**

Read the words in the box. Listen for the vowel sound in each word.

bike	tie	try	time	fright
find	cry	right	fly	high
why	might	side	bright	like

The words from the box are shown below. Shapes are where the letters that stand for the vowel sounds should be. Write the words with the right letters in place of the shapes.

1. fl★ _____

2. t❤◆ _____

3. r❤■●t _____

4. f❤nd _____

5. cr★ _____

6. wh★ _____

7. m❤■●t _____

8. s❤d◆ _____

9. h❤■● _____

10. b❤k◆ _____

11. t❤m◆ _____

12. fr❤■●t _____

13. tr★ _____

14. br❤■●t _____

15. l❤k◆ _____

Name _____ Date _____

Vowel Sounds: /o-e/, /o/, /oe/, /oa/

 The vowel sound you hear in the word <u>bone</u> can be spelled four ways.

<u>o</u>-consonant-<u>e</u> as in <u>rope</u>   <u>o</u> as in <u>open</u>

<u>ow</u> as in <u>shadow</u>   <u>oa</u> as in <u>goat</u>

✏️ **Practice**

Read the words in the box. Listen for the vowel sound in each word.

coat	troll	blow	so	go	home
bowl	nose	boat	oh	snow	low
toad	old	grow	road	bone	cold

The words from the box are shown below. Spaces are where the letters that stand for the vowel sounds should be. Finish the words by writing the correct letters in the spaces.

1. b _____ _____ t

2. h _____ m _____

3. _____ h

4. sn _____ _____

5. g _____

6. bl _____ _____

7. _____ ld

8. b _____ n _____

9. t _____ _____ d

10. n _____ s _____

11. l _____ _____

12. tr _____ ll

13. s _____

14. b _____ _____ l

15. c _____ _____ t

16. gr _____ _____

17. c _____ ld

18. r _____ _____ d

Vowel Sounds: /u–e/

☞ The vowel sound you hear in the word <u>cute</u> can be spelled this way.

<u>u</u>-consonant-<u>e</u> as in <u>use</u>

☞ The vowel sound you hear in the word <u>tube</u> can be spelled this way.

<u>u</u>-consonant-<u>e</u> as in <u>dune</u>

✏ **Practice**

Finish each sentence. Write the word that makes sense in the sentence.

1. The girl sang a happy _____.

     time   team   tune

2. The ice _____ is cold.

     cube   cut   cub

3. The _____ for the lamp does not work.

     fuss   fuse   face

4. What is your _____ for being late?

     excuse   escape   excite

5. Squeeze the toothpaste from the _____.

     tub   tame   tube

6. We saw a sand _____ at the beach.

     done   dune   did

7. The elephant is a _____ animal.

     home   hug   huge

Name _____ Date _____

Vowel Sounds: /o/, /oo/, /ew/, /ou/

☞ The vowel sound you hear in the word <u>food</u> can be spelled
four ways.

<u>o</u> as in <u>two</u>
<u>oo</u> as in <u>boot</u>
<u>ew</u> as in <u>blew</u>
<u>ou</u> as in <u>soup</u>

✎ **Practice**

Read the words in the box. Listen for the vowel sound in each word.

who	tool	goose	zoo
room	moon	group	chew

1. I am an animal.
   What am I? _____

2. I am a question word.
   What am I? _____

3. I help make things.
   What am I? _____

4. I am a set of things.
   What am I? _____

5. I tell what teeth do.
   What am I? _____

6. I am a home for animals.
   What am I? _____

7. I shine at night.
   What am I? _____

8. I am in a house.
   What am I? _____

Vowel Sounds: /or/, /ore/, /oor/, /ar/

☞ The vowel sound you hear in the word <u>horn</u> can be spelled four ways.

or as in <u>horn</u>
ore as in <u>more</u>
oor as in <u>door</u>
ar as in <u>warm</u>

 Practice

Read the words in the box. Listen to the vowel sound in each word.

floor	corn	horse	warn	more
shore	torn	north	store	sport

The words from the box are shown below. Shapes are where the letters that stand for vowel sounds should be. Write the words with the right letters in place of the shapes.

1. sh■●▲ _____

2. t■●n _____

3. st■●▲ _____

4. sp■●t _____

5. fl■■● _____

6. c■●n _____

7. h■●se _____

8. w◆●n _____

9. m■●▲ _____

10. n■●th _____

Name _____   Date _____

Vowel Sounds: /ear/, /er/, /or/, /ur/, /ir/

☞ The vowel sound you hear in the word <u>search</u> can be spelled five ways.

<u>ear</u> as in <u>heard</u>   **<u>er</u> as in <u>her</u>**   **<u>or</u> as in <u>word</u>**
<u>ur</u> as in <u>turnip</u>   **<u>ir</u> as in <u>girl</u>**

✏ **Practice**

Read the words in the box. Listen to the vowel sound in each word.

earth	work	skirt	burn	hurt
first	learn	serve	bird	world

The words from the box are shown below. Spaces are where the letters that stand for vowel sounds should be. Finish the words by writing the correct letters in the spaces.

1. b ____ ____ d

2. ____ ____ ____ th

3. s ____ ____ ve

4. w ____ ____ ld

5. h ____ ____ t

6. f ____ ____ st

7. sk ____ ____ t

8. b ____ ____ n

9. w ____ ____ k

10. l ____ ____ ____ n

Finish the sentence with words from the box.

11. The _____ flew to its nest.

12. The hot sun can _____ your skin.

13. Ann wears a pretty blue _____ .

14. You can _____ how to spell words.

Language Arts 2, SV 3888-3

Name _____ Date _____

Vowel Sounds: /ar/, /are/, /air/, /ear/, /eer/

☞ The vowel sound you hear in the word <u>start</u> can be spelled this way.

<u>ar</u> as in <u>yarn</u>

☞ The vowel sound you hear in the word <u>hair</u> can be spelled three ways.

<u>are</u> as in <u>care</u>   <u>air</u> as in <u>chair</u>
<u>ear</u> as in <u>bear</u>

☞ The vowel sound you hear in the word <u>cheer</u> can be spelled two ways.

<u>eer</u> as in <u>cheer</u>   <u>ear</u> as in <u>dear</u>

 **Practice**

Say the name for each picture. Listen to each vowel sound. Write words from the box that have the same vowel sound under each picture. Write words with the same vowel sound under each other.

hard	wear	clear	dark
cart	care	hair	dare
fair	steer	near	pear

1.   **2.**   **3.**

_____   _____   _____

_____   _____   _____

_____   _____   _____

_____

_____

Name _____ Date _____

Vowel Sounds: /er/, /or/, /ar/

 The vowel sounds you hear at the end of the word <u>mother</u> can be spelled three ways.

er as in **<u>summer</u>**   **or** as in **<u>tractor</u>**
ar as in **<u>collar</u>**

✎ **Practice**

Read each word in the box. Listen for the vowel sound at the end of each word. All the words in the box have the vowel sound you hear at the end of the word <u>mother</u>.

winter	sweater	flower	supper
father	motor	dollar	river
color	feather		

Read each set of words. Find the word in the box that goes with the other words in the set. Write the word on the line.

1. spring, summer, ____winter____

2. hat, coat, _____

3. lake, stream, _____

4. power, engine, _____

5. mother, sister, _____

6. penny, nickel, _____

7. breakfast, lunch, _____

8. wing, beak, _____

9. rose, daisy, _____

10. draw, paint, _____

Name _____ Date _____

Vowel Sounds: /ou/, /ow/, /oi/, /oy/

☞ The vowel sound you hear in the word <u>ground</u> can be spelled two ways.

<u>ou</u> as in <u>about</u>

<u>ow</u> as in <u>tower</u>

☞ The vowel sound you hear in the word <u>voice</u> can be spelled two ways.

<u>oi</u> as in <u>join</u>

<u>oy</u> as in <u>boy</u>

 Practice

Say the name for each picture. Listen to each vowel sound. Write words from the box that have the same vowel sound next to each picture. Write words with the same sound under each other.

joy	loud	out	toy	how
coin	point	choice	pound	town

1.

_____

_____

_____

_____

2.

_____

_____

_____

_____

Language Arts 2, SV 3888-3

Name _____ Date _____

Unit Two Assessment: Grammar

✏ Write <u>noun</u>, <u>verb</u>, <u>adjective</u>, <u>pronoun</u>, <u>compound word</u>, or <u>contraction</u> to name each underlined word.

☞
> **Remember:**
> •Noun: a person, place, or thing
> •Verb: a word that shows action, or a word that tells about being
> •Adjective: a describing word
> •Pronoun: a word that takes the place of one or more nouns
> •Compound word: two words put together to make a new word
> •Contraction: two words put together with an apostrophe taking the place of one or more letters

1. My grandmother has <u>green</u> eyes. _____

2. We <u>ran</u> all the way home. _____

3. His <u>house</u> is the white one. _____

4. <u>She</u> can come with me. _____

5. <u>Can't</u> you hear the ocean? _____

6. I will not <u>be</u> here long. _____

7. We live on <u>Main Street</u>. _____

8. My <u>birthday</u> has come and gone. _____

9. I did not know <u>they</u> were coming. _____

10. It <u>isn't</u> fair to eat it all. _____

11. My sister <u>falls</u> down often. _____

12. The teacher never <u>goes</u> in there. _____

13. There are <u>twelve</u> houses on my street. _____

14. I can't find my <u>sunglasses</u>. _____

15. That is the <u>tallest</u> tree I have ever seen. _____

Nouns

☞ A **noun** is a word that names a person, place, or thing.

A <u>girl</u> went walking.
She went to the <u>store</u>.
She bought a <u>sausage</u>.

✎ **Practice**

Read the sentences. Underline the nouns. Tell if each noun names a person, place, or thing.

1. Why is this house so funny?   _____

2. Look what is on the ceiling.   _____

3. The closet is full.   _____

4. Watch out for the flying hat!   _____

5. That shoe is walking!   _____

6. Will the boy find it?   _____

Read the sentences. Add nouns. You may choose words from the box.

| floor | woman | song | girl | man | store |

7. A little _____ walked down the street.

8. She went into a _____.

9. Then she whistled a _____.

10. She danced on the _____.

11. The _____ looked surprised.

12. The _____ looked through the window.

36

Name _____ Date _____

Names and Titles of People and Places

☞ The names of people are special nouns. The first and last names of a person begin with a capital letter.

<u>Jack Sprat</u> went to the airport.

☞ The titles of people begin with a capital letter. Most titles end with a period.

<u>Mrs.</u> Sprat is looking for her son.

These are titles of people.

Mr.   Mrs.   Ms.   Dr.   Miss

☞ Cities, states, and names of streets begin with a capital letter.

Jack saw his friends in <u>Florida</u>.

Their house is at 212 <u>Coconut Drive</u>.

✏ **Practice**

Write the sentences correctly. Add capital letters.

1. Where did jack sprat go?

_____

2. mary saw her friend jill.

_____

3. Did mr. or mrs. sprat go with them?

_____

4. They met ms. muffet along the way.

_____

5. They walked along michigan avenue.

_____

6. Then they drove through indiana and ohio.

_____

Days of the Week, Months, and Holidays

☞   The names of the days of the week are special nouns. They begin with capital letters.

The man flew in a spaceship on <u>Saturday</u>.

☞   The names of the months are also special nouns. They begin with capital letters.

In <u>December </u>he drives in the snow.

☞   The names of holidays are special nouns. Each important word in the name of the holiday begins with a capital letter.

He had a picnic on the <u>Fourth of July</u>.

✎ **Practice**

Write the sentences. Use the words from the box. Find the day, month, or holiday that begins with the same letter as the underlined word.

Wednesday   February   Saturday   Thanksgiving   July

1. Francis Foley did not <u>walk</u> on _____.

2. He <u>flew</u> in _____.

3. Sometimes he <u>sails</u> on _____.

4. He <u>jumped</u> up and down in _____.

5. He <u>thinks</u> he will be home for _____.

Name _____   Date _____

One or More Than One

☞   A noun is a word that names a person, place, or thing.

One <u>girl</u> wears a black <u>hat</u>.

☞   A noun can tell about more than one person, place, or thing.
Add <u>s</u> to most nouns to make them mean "more than one."

Many <u>boys</u> wear funny <u>masks</u>.

✏ **Practice**

Choose and circle the correct nouns.

1. Two (boy, boys) went out on Halloween.

2. A (girl, girls) walked with them.

3. She wore a black (robe, robes).

4. There were two red (star, stars) on it.

5. It also had one orange (moon, moons).

6. The children walked up to a (house, houses).

7. Then they knocked on the (door, doors).

8. Will they ask for some (treat, treats)?

9. Then the children saw two (cat, cats).

10. Two (dog, dogs) ran down the street.

11. An (owl, owls) hooted in the darkness.

12. Many (star, stars) were in the sky.

13. The wind blew through all the (tree, trees).

14. The children clapped their (hand, hands).

15. Then they sang a (song, songs).

Name _____ Date _____

Verbs

☞ An **action verb** is a word that shows action.

People <u>drive</u> across the country.
We <u>walk</u> to school.

✏️ **Practice**

A. Read the sentences. Add an action verb from the box to each sentence.

ride	run	take	jog	climb
travel	fly	zoom	visit	drive

1. People _____ to many places.

2. Sometimes they _____ in cars.

3. The boys _____ their friends.

4. They _____ on the train.

5. Some trains _____ up hills.

6. Bicycles _____ people to interesting places.

7. Some people _____ in races.

8. They _____ down the street.

9. Planes _____ into the sky.

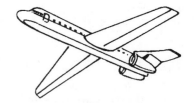

10. Rockets _____ into space.

B. Finish the story. Add action verbs. You may choose words from the box above.

The children _____ their bicycles everywhere. They _____ up big hills. Sometimes they pretend to be pilots. Then they _____ into the sky.

Name _____ Date _____

Verbs

☞ Add <u>s</u> to an action verb that tells about one person or thing.

The pirate <u>walks</u> quickly.
He <u>sees</u> his friends.

✎ **Practice**

Read the sentences. Choose and circle the correct verbs.

1. The cat (skip, skips) down the steps.

2. Two cats (play, plays) on the stairs.

3. The children (hug, hugs) the cat.

4. The cat (purr, purrs) happily.

5. A puppy (bark, barks) at the cat.

6. The boys (hide, hides) from the girls.

7. An ape (wave, waves) to them.

8. The wind (blows, blow) the trees.

9. My shadow (follow, follows) me.

10. A girl (sees, see) a shadow.

11. The pirate (jump, jumps) over the fence.

12. Mary (hear, hears) the tree speak.

13. The branches (move, moves) in the wind.

14. An owl (hoot, hoots) in the tree.

15. The children (take, takes) their treats home.

16. They (eat, eats) some fruit.

17. Sam (chew, chews) an apple.

18. The dog (beg, begs) for a treat.

Verbs in the Present Tense

☞ Verbs can tell about action that happens now.

Max and Lisa <u>walk</u> to school.

☞ Add <u>s</u> to an action verb that tells about
one person or thing.

Lisa <u>walks</u> to school.

 **Practice**

A. Read the sentences. Choose and circle the correct verbs.

1. Max (play, plays) baseball.

2. He (run, runs) fast.

3. The girls (dance, dances) to the music.

4. Some friends (wait, waits) for Max.

5. Lisa (leap, leaps) across the floor.

B. Finish the story. Add action verbs. You may use words from
the box.

sits	leaps	asks
takes	walks	hits

　　　Max _____ his sister to her dancing class. He

_____ on a chair to watch. The teacher_____ him

to join the class. First, he _____ off his sneakers. Then he

_____ to the park. Last, he _____ a home run.

Name _____ Date _____

Verbs in the Past Tense

☞ Verbs can tell about actions in the past. Form the **past tense** of most verbs by adding <u>ed</u>.

Mary Jo <u>planted</u> vegetables yesterday.

✐ **Practice**

Make each sentence tell about the past. Choose and circle the correct verb.

1. Jeff (plays, played) with his sister.

2. The family (visited, visits) Grandmother often.

3. Mary Jo (looks, looked) out the window.

4. Then she (jumped, jumps) up and down.

5. Grandmother (leans, leaned) back on the pillow.

Find the verbs. Then write each verb in the past tense.

6. Mary Jo walks to the creek.   _____

7. Grandmother laughs at the baby chicks. _____

8. Mary Jo wants a warm biscuit.   _____

9. Mary Jo opens the oven door.   _____

10. She pours some milk.   _____

11. Grandmother walks down the stairs.   _____

12. Mary Jo helps Grandmother.   _____

Name _____ Date _____

Verbs That Do Not Show Action

☞ Some verbs do not show action. They tell about being.

A snake is a reptile.

The snake was hungry.

☞ Verbs can tell about being now or being in the past.

Now	**Past**
am, is, are	was, were

☞ Use <u>am</u> or <u>was</u> with the word <u>I</u>.

I <u>am</u> in the tree.   **I <u>was</u> under the tree.**

☞ Use <u>is</u> or <u>was</u> with one person or thing. Use <u>are</u> or <u>were</u> with more than one person or thing.

A lizard <u>is</u> in my garden.

Two turtles <u>were</u> in a box.

✎ **Practice**

Read the sentences. Choose and circle the correct verbs.

1. Reptiles (are, is) cold-blooded animals.

2. Some snakes (are, is) dangerous.

3. Many kinds of lizards (were, was) at the zoo.

4. A draco (is, am) a lizard.

5. Crocodiles (are, is) the largest reptiles.

6. The crocodiles (were, was) very noisy.

7. One lizard (is, are) in the box.

8. I (is, am) near the turtle's box.

9. The box (was, were) near the window.

10. The turtle (is, are) sleeping.

Name _____ Date _____

Verbs That Do Not Show Action

☞ Some verbs do not show action.

A snake <u>has</u> no eyelids.

☞ Verbs can tell about now and the past.

Now	**Past**
have, has	had

☞ Use <u>have</u> with the word <u>I</u>.

I <u>have</u> a turtle.

☞ Use <u>has</u> with one person or thing. Use <u>have</u> with more than one person or thing.

A crocodile <u>has</u> a long snout.

Crocodiles <u>have</u> strong jaws.

✏ **Practice**

Read the sentences. Choose and circle the correct verbs.

1. A tuatara (has, have) three eyelids.

2. Reptiles (has, have) backbones.

3. Last year, I (have, had) a lizard for a pet.

4. The alligator (has, have) a short snout.

5. These tortoises (has, have) new shells.

Finish each sentence. Use <u>has</u> or <u>have</u>.

6. Reptiles _____ scales.

7. A snake _____ dry, smooth skin.

8. Mary and Jack _____ a pet turtle.

9. The lizard _____ a new tail.

10. My friends _____ a book about lizards.

© Steck-Vaughn Company

Other Verbs

☞ Some action verbs do not add <u>ed</u> to tell about the past.

The animals <u>ran</u> into the woods.
The men <u>went</u> to sleep.
A dog <u>came</u> to a farm.

☞ Verbs can tell about now and the past.

Now	Past
go, goes	went
come, comes	came
run, runs	ran

 Practice

Read the sentences. Choose and circle the correct verbs.

1. Three robbers (ran, runs) out the door.

2. They (comes, came) back.

3. Four animals (goes, went) by the house.

4. The rooster and the dog (go, goes) into the kitchen.

5. The friends (run, runs) down the road.

6. A cat (goes, go) very fast.

Find the verb in each sentence. Write each verb in the past tense.

7. The man goes to the mill. _____

8. A donkey comes to town. _____

9. The animals come to a big house. _____

10. They run to the window. _____

Adjectives

☞ An **adjective** is a describing word. A describing word describes a noun.

The <u>old</u> woman walked home.

☞ Describing words can tell about color.

<u>Red</u> flowers grow in the garden.

☞ Describing words can tell about size.

The woman lives in a <u>tiny</u> house.

☞ Describing words can tell about shape.

The house has a <u>square</u> window.

☞ Describing words can tell how something feels, tastes, sounds, or smells.

The flowers have a <u>sweet</u> smell.

✎ Practice

Finish the sentences. Add describing words from the box.

round	long	brown	tiny	pink	juicy

1. The woman puts on a _____ bonnet.

2. She walks down a _____ road.

3. _____ squirrels run by.

4. A man gives her a _____ orange.

5. The orange is _____.

6. Do you see a _____ bone in the yard?

Adjectives

Adjectives are describing words.

☞ Describing words can describe feelings.

The woman was <u>surprised</u>.

She was <u>happy</u>.

☞ Describing words can also tell how many.

She picked <u>four</u> flowers.

☞ Some describing words that tell how many do not tell exact numbers.

There are <u>many</u> roses in the garden.

<u>Some</u> grass grows here.

✏ Practice

Finish the sentences. Add describing words from the box.

happy	hungry	three	one
some	tired	sleepy	many

1. The woman was _____ from walking so far.

2. She was _____ to be home.

3. First, she put _____ flowers in a vase.

4. Next, she put _____ bone in a pot.

5. She was _____ and wanted to eat.

6. Then, she ate _____ soup.

7. She also had _____ crackers.

8. Last, the woman was _____ and went to bed.

Name _____   Date _____

Adjectives That Compare

☞ Add <u>er</u> to most describing words when they are used to compare two things.

This tree is <u>bigger</u> than that one.

☞ Add <u>est</u> to most describing words when they are used to compare more than two things.

The sequoia tree is the <u>biggest</u> tree of all.

 Practice

Read the chart. Fill in the missing describing words.

1. long	longer	longest
2. bright	_____	brightest
3. tall	taller	_____
4. _____	faster	fastest

Read the sentences. Choose and circle the correct describing words.

5. That tree trunk is (thick, thicker) than this one.

6. The giant sequoia is the (bigger, biggest) living thing of all.

7. The stump of a giant sequoia is (wider, widest) than my room.

8. These trees are the (older, oldest) of all.

Name _____ Date _____

Pronouns

☞ A **pronoun** is a word that takes the place of one or more nouns.

> **The mouse and the lion are friends.**
> **They are friends.**

☞ The pronouns I, we, he, she, it, and they are used in the naming part of a sentence.

> **The mouse helped the lion.**
> **She helped the lion.**

 **Practice**

Read the sentences. Think of a pronoun for the underlined words. Write the pronoun on the line.

1. The mouse and I live in the woods. _____

2. The mouse fell into the spring. _____

3. The lion saw the mouse fall. _____

4. The leaf landed in the water. _____

5. A hunter spread a net. _____

6. The net was for the lion. _____

7. The mouse and the lion helped each other. _____

8. The mouse and I will always be friends. _____

9. The mouse and the lion are happy. _____

10. The mouse and I will watch out for the hunter. _____

Compound Words

☞ Sometimes two words can be put together to make a new word. The new word is called a **compound word**.

> **lunch + room = lunchroom**
>
> **every + day = everyday**

  Practice

Write compound words. Pick words from Box 1 and Box 2.
Write the new word in Box 3.

Box 1	Box 2	Box 3
1. sun	noon	_____
2. after	glasses	_____
3. play	side	_____
4. birth	ground	_____
5. out	book	_____
6. scrap	day	_____

Finish the sentences. You may use some of the compound words you made above.

7. Dana is wearing _____ in class.

8. Dana and Brad eat together on the _____.

9. Then they play _____.

10. In the _____, Dana was sent to the principal's office.

11. Brad put a picture of the school in his _____.

12. Brad will be eight years old on his next _____.

Name _____ Date _____

Contractions

☞ A **contraction** is a way to put words together.

is + not = isn't

☞ An **apostrophe** takes the place of one or more letters. In these contractions, the letter <u>o</u> is left out of the word <u>not</u>. A contraction is written as one word.

is + not = isn't	**was + not = wasn't**
are + not = aren't	**were + not = weren't**
have + not = haven't	**had + not = hadn't**
has + not = hasn't	**can + not = can't**
did + not = didn't	**do + not = don't**

✎ **Practice**

Read the sentences. Think of a contraction to use in place of the underlined words. Write the contraction on the line.

1. George <u>is not</u> fond of tomato soup.   _____

2. Poor George <u>cannot</u> stand another bowl.   _____

3. George <u>had not</u> really eaten the soup.   _____

4. The soup <u>was not</u> so bad.   _____

5. Carla and George <u>have not</u> eaten anything else.   _____

6. George <u>did not</u> tell Carla.   _____

7. I <u>do not</u> like tomato soup.   _____

8. Carla <u>has not</u> made soup today.   _____

Name _____ Date _____

Unit Three Assessment: Sentences

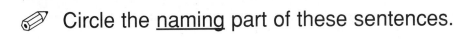 Circle the <u>naming</u> part of these sentences.

1. Bear went for a walk.

2. The tree is tall and green.

3. That ride was lots of fun.

 Circle the <u>action</u> part of these sentences.

4. My friends and I ran to the store.

5. Flowers grow in my garden.

6. Yesterday, I mailed three letters.

✏ Write whether each sentence is an <u>asking sentence</u>, a <u>statement</u>, or an <u>exclamation</u>.

7. The seeds are starting to grow. _____

8. Can you see the little green stems? _____

9. They are an inch tall already! _____

✏ Write a joining sentence for each pair of sentences.

10. I planted some seeds. I watered the seeds.

_____

11. The flowers grew. The flowers were pretty.

_____

✏ Write a better sentence. Add a describing word and replace the underlined verb with a more exact verb.

12. The train <u>went</u> by me on the tracks.

_____

Sentences and Sentence Parts

☞ A **sentence** is a group of words that tells a complete thought. Every sentence begins with a capital letter. Every sentence ends with a mark.

John works in his garden.

☞ Every sentence has two parts. The **naming part** tells who or what the sentence is about.

☞ The **action part** tells something about the naming part. A naming part and an action part make a complete thought.

Naming Part   **Action Part**
Sara   plants some seeds.

 **Practice**

Each group of words needs a naming part or an action part. Add words to make each group of words a complete sentence.

1. John _____.

2. Sara _____.

3. _____ need sun and rain.

4. The flower seeds _____.

5. John and Sara _____.

6. _____ looks at the flower.

7. _____ grow in the garden.

Kinds of Sentences

☞ A **statement** is a sentence that tells something. It begins with a capital letter. It ends with a **period(.)**.

John gives some seeds to Sara.

☞ A **question** is a sentence that asks something. It begins with a capital letter. It ends with a **question mark (?)**.

Will Sara plant seeds?

☞ An **exclamation** is a sentence that shows strong feeling. It begins with a capital letter. It ends with an **exclamation point (!)**.

What a fine garden John has!

✏ **Practice**

Read the sentences. Write <u>statement</u> for a telling sentence. Write <u>question</u> for an asking sentence. Write <u>exclamation</u> for a sentence that shows strong feeling.

1. John was in his garden. _____

2. Who came walking by? _____

3. Sara stopped to look at the garden. _____

4. What did Sara do? _____

5. Sara read a story to her seeds. _____

6. Did Sara do anything else? _____

7. Poor Sara fell asleep in her garden! _____

8. The seeds started to grow. _____

9. What makes seeds grow? _____

10. Sara works so hard! _____

Name _____   Date _____

Joining Sentences

☞ A writer can join two short sentences. This makes the sentences more interesting to read. The word <u>and</u> is used to join the sentences.

☞ Sometimes the naming parts of two sentences are the same. The action parts can be joined.

John planted seeds. John worked in his garden.
John planted seeds <u>and</u> worked in his garden.

How to Join Sentences
1. Look for sentences that have the same naming part.
2. Write the naming part.
3. Look for different action parts. Use the word <u>and</u> to join them.
4. Write the new sentence.

✏ **Practice**

Join each pair of sentences. Write new sentences. Use the word <u>and</u>.

1. John gave seeds to Sara.
    John told her to plant them.

    _____

2. Sara planted the seeds.
    Sara looked at the ground.

    _____

3. Sara sang songs to her seeds.
    Sara read stories to them.

    _____

4. The rain fell on the seeds.
    The rain helped them grow.

    _____

Joining Sentences

☞ A writer can join two short sentences. This makes the sentences more interesting to read. The word <u>and</u> is used to join the sentences.

☞ Sometimes the action parts of two sentences are the same. Then the naming parts can be joined.

The hunter stopped at the house.
The bear stopped at the house.
The hunter <u>and</u> the bear stopped at the house.

How to Join Sentences

1. Look for sentences that have the same action part.
2. Join the naming parts. Use the word <u>and.</u>
3. Add the action part.

✐ **Practice**

Join each pair of sentences. Write new sentences. Use the word <u>and</u>.

1. The farmer stood in the doorway.
   His family stood in the doorway.

   _____

2. The hunter stayed with the family.
   The bear stayed with the family.

   _____

3. The mice ran out the door.
   The children ran out the door.

   _____

4. The hunter went home.
   The bear went home.

   _____

Adding Describing Words to Sentences

☞ A writer adds describing words to sentences to give a clear picture.

The moth sat on top of a clover.
The moth sat on top of a <u>white</u> clover.

How to Add Describing Words to Sentences

1. Look for sentences that do not give your reader a clear picture.
2. Think of describing words that tell more about what things look like.
3. Add the describing words to the sentences.

✎ **Practice**

Make these sentences give a clearer picture. Add describing words. Write the new sentences.

1. Sam is a moth.

_____

2. Can Sam feel the breeze?

_____

3. The pond was Sam's place.

_____

4. The children put Sam in a jar.

_____

5. Sam flew back to the pond.

_____

Beginning Sentences in Different Ways

☞ A writer does not begin every sentence with the same noun. Sometimes the words <u>he</u>, <u>she</u>, <u>I</u>, <u>we</u>, and <u>they</u> are used in place of nouns.

Ant climbed down a branch. Ant was thirsty. <u>She</u> tried to get a drink.

How to Begin Sentences in Different Ways

1. Look for sentences that begin with the same noun.

2. Use the word <u>he</u>, <u>she</u>, <u>I</u>, <u>we</u>, or <u>they</u> in place of the noun.

3. Write the new sentence.

✎ **Practice**

Make these sentences more interesting. Begin some of them with <u>he</u>, <u>she</u>, <u>I</u>, <u>we</u>, or <u>they</u>. Write the new sentences.

1. The ant climbed down a blade of grass. The ant fell into the spring.

_____

2. The bird pulled off a leaf. The bird let the leaf fall into the water.

_____

3. The hunter saw a lion. The hunter spread his net.

_____

4. The lion and I live in the woods. The lion and I are friends.

_____

Name _____ Date _____

Writing Clear Sentences

☞ A writer uses exact verbs. These are verbs that give a clear picture of an action.

Spaceships <u>go</u> to the moon.
Spaceships <u>zoom</u> to the moon.

How to Use Exact Verbs in Sentences

1. Picture the action. Think about what a person or thing is doing.
2. Choose an action verb. Tell exactly what the person or thing is doing.
3. Use the action verb in a sentence.

✏ **Practice**

Make each sentence give a clearer picture. Think of a more exact verb for each underlined verb. Then write the new word on the line.

1. People <u>walk</u> to work. _____

2. Trains <u>move</u> along the tracks. _____

3. We <u>ride</u> our bicycles. _____

4. Fast cars <u>go</u> up the road. _____

5. The airplane <u>flies</u> in the sky. _____

6. A man <u>runs</u> around the park. _____

7. The children <u>walk</u> to school. _____

8. A bus <u>goes</u> down the highway. _____

Name _____ Date _____

Unit Four Assessment: Vocabulary and Usage

✎ Choose a word from the box that means almost the same thing as the underlined word. Write the word in the blank.

wonderful	house	tune

1. My <u>home</u> is on this street. _____

2. This is my favorite <u>song</u>. _____

3. That movie was <u>great</u>. _____

✎ Choose a word from the box that means the opposite of the underlined words.

found	worst	close

4. Hurry and <u>open</u> the door. _____

5. I <u>lost</u> the book I was reading. _____

6. This was the <u>best</u> day of the week. _____

✎ Circle the <u>prefix</u> or <u>suffix</u> in each word.

7. unable   **9.** mistake   **11.** breakable

8. clearly   **10.** hopeless   **12.** return

✎ Choose one word from the box to complete each sentence. Write the word in the blank.

to	too	two	there
their	they're	I	me

13. I want to go _____.

14. I like _____ yard.

15. Please come with _____.

16. My family has _____ cars.

17. Park them over _____.

Name _____   Date _____

Synonyms

☞ **Synonyms** are words that mean almost the same thing.

My <u>hat</u> is in the closet.
My <u>cap</u> is in the closet.

✏️ **Practice**

Write new sentences. Change the underlined word. Use a word from the box that means almost the same thing.

seat	home	plates	couch

1. I have a silly <u>house</u>.   _____

2. The <u>sofa</u> is on the ceiling.   _____

3. A <u>chair</u> is on the wall.   _____

4. <u>Dishes</u> fly around the room.   _____

Read each sentence about a silly house. Then finish the second sentence. Choose the word in ( ) that means almost the same thing as the underlined word and write it in the blank.

5. My <u>friend</u> and I are in my room. My _____ looks in my closet. (mother, pal)

6. My <u>hat</u> flies through the window. I catch the _____ and put it on. (cap, sock)

7. My <u>rug</u> rolls up by itself. We unroll the _____ and make it flat. (paper, carpet)

8. My friend and I make up a silly <u>tune</u>. We will sing the _____ together. (song, words)

Language Arts 2, SV 3888-3

Name _____ Date _____

Antonyms

☞ **Antonyms** are words with opposite meanings.

      I feel <u>sad</u>.
      My mother feels <u>happy</u>.

✎ **Practice**

Read the sentences. Underline the two words that mean the opposite.

1. I am wearing a new jacket and an old hat.

2. I run down the stairs and up the hill.

3. I go to school in the day and help my mother at night.

4. My mother is tall, but I am short.

5. My mother puts a big meal on a little plate.

Make new sentences. Choose a word from the box that means the opposite of each underlined word. Write it on the line.

late	walk	down	dry
close	cool	sunny	

6. I awake <u>early</u> in the morning. _____

7. I look <u>up</u>. _____

8. I <u>open</u> the window. _____

9. Then I <u>run</u> into the woods. _____

10. The ground is <u>wet</u>. _____

11. The air is <u>warm</u>. _____

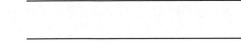

12. The day is <u>cloudy</u>. _____

Name _____ Date _____

Prefixes

☞ A **prefix** is a group of letters added to the beginning of a word. Adding a prefix to a word changes its meaning.

The old woman was <u>happy</u>.
The old woman was <u>unhappy</u>.

Prefix	Meaning	Example
un	not	unclear
re	again	rewrite

✎ **Practice**

Read the sentences. Underline each word that has a prefix. Tell the meaning of the word.

1. The old man was unable to find something to wear. _____

2. The old woman reopened the drawer. _____

3. She told the old man they were unlucky. _____

4. The old man felt this was unfair. _____

5. He was very unhappy. _____

6. The woman asked the man to rewind the yarn. _____

7. The old woman rewashed the socks. _____

8. Could the socks be uneven? _____

9. The old man refilled his wife's glass. _____

10. The farmer's wife reknitted the sweater. _____

Name _____   Date _____

Suffixes

☞ A **suffix** is a group of letters added to the end of a word.
Adding a suffix to a word changes its meaning.

Josef's parents were <u>helpless</u>.
The doctor was <u>helpful</u>.

Suffix	Meaning	Example
ful	full of	hopeful
less	without	useless
able	able to be	breakable

✎ **Practice**

Read the sentences. Underline each word that has a suffix. Tell the
meaning of each word.

1. Josef's mother wanted him to be cheerful. _____

2. Is Josef careful? _____

3. Josef thought the game was harmless. _____

4. The chair Josef was on was breakable. _____

5. Is the chair useless now? _____

Read the sentences. Add a word from the box. Tell the meaning of
the word you chose.

hopeful	dreadful	thankful

6. Josef's parents had a _____ shock! _____

7. They were _____ the chair would not break. _____

8. When Josef came out of the hospital, he was very

   _____. _____

Name _____ Date _____

Troublesome Words

☞ Use <u>to</u> when you mean "in the direction of."
Some dinosaurs go <u>to</u> the lake.

☞ Use <u>too</u> when you mean "also."
Did the bird go, <u>too</u>?

☞ Use <u>two</u> when you mean "one more than one."
<u>**Two**</u> **dinosaurs are eating the plants.**

✏ **Practice**

Finish each sentence. Add the word <u>to</u>, <u>too</u>, or <u>two</u>.

1. These _____ dinosaurs were fat.

2. The dinosaur ate meat, _____.

3. Did the dinosaurs go _____ the desert?

4. Brontosaurus had a tiny mouth, _____.

5. This dinosaur ran _____ the swamp.

6. Can you find _____ dinosaurs in the picture?

7. Pentaceratops had more than _____ horns.

8. Tyrannosaurus had huge jaws, _____.

9. That small dinosaur went _____ the tree.

10. People have found dinosaur teeth, _____.

11. My brother has _____ pictures of dinosaurs in his room.

12. I read a story about dinosaurs _____ him.

13. My brother liked the story, _____.

14. Then he went _____ the library.

15. He got _____ more books about dinosaurs.

Name _____ Date _____

Troublesome Words

☞ Use <u>there</u> when you mean "in that place."
The dinosaur is over <u>there</u>.

☞ Use <u>their</u> when you mean "belonging to them."
This is <u>their</u> swamp.

☞ <u>They're</u> is a contraction for <u>they are</u>. Use <u>they're</u> when you mean "they are."
<u>They're</u> eating leaves from the trees.

✏ **Practice**

Read the sentences. Choose and circle the correct words.

1. Is this (their, they're) food?

2. (There, They're) huge animals.

3. Pentaceratops is over (there, their).

4. Once it was (there, their) land.

5. Dinosaurs lived (they're, there) for a while.

6. (They're, There) everywhere!

7. (They're, There) the two biggest dinosaurs.

8. The faster dinosaur is resting (their, there).

9. Small dinosaurs lived (they're, there) long ago.

10. (Their, There) land was different then.

11. I see some more dinosaurs over (they're, there).

12. (They're, There) in the lake.

Troublesome Words

☞ The word <u>I</u> is always used in the naming part of a sentence. <u>I</u> is always written with a capital letter.

> **<u>I</u> go to school.**

☞ When you speak of or write about another person and yourself, always name yourself last.

> **Tina and <u>I</u> are in the same class.**

☞ The word <u>me</u> follows an action verb.

> **Tina makes <u>me</u> laugh.**
>
> **The teacher tells Tina and <u>me</u> to be quiet.**

✐ Practice

Finish each sentence correctly. Use <u>I</u> or <u>me</u>.

1. _____ am taking a test.

2. The teacher tells _____ to stop laughing.

3. Mother takes _____ home.

4. _____ have fun with Tina.

Read the sentences. Choose and circle the correct words.

5. (Susan and I, I and Susan) are friends.

6. The teacher tells (Tina and me, me and Tina) to hush.

7. (I and Tina, Tina and I) eat lunch together.

8. Mr. Smith asks (Susan and me, Susan and I) to pass out the papers.

Tues. HW

Name _____   Date _____

Unit Five Assessment: Capitalization and Punctuation

✏ Write each sentence again. Use capital letters correctly and add missing punctuation marks—periods, question marks, exclamation points, commas, and apostrophes.

1. my uncle john likes to have a garden.

_____

2. he lives on Smith street

_____

3. can you come with me on tuesday june 3

_____

4. i am reading a book called great gardens.

_____

5. it has pictures of giant plants

_____

6. mr lopez lives near my uncle

_____

7. dont you think it would be nice to visit him

_____

8. in august, the garden will have many vegetables

_____

Sentences

☞ Begin the first word of a sentence with a capital letter.

The garden is very pretty.
Flowers grow there.
What kind of flowers do you see?

✐ **Practice**

Read each sentence. Circle the letters that should be capital letters.

1. there are many kinds of gardens.

2. flowers grow in some gardens.

3. vegetables grow in other gardens.

4. green grass grows around some gardens.

5. you can find gardens in parks.

6. many people have gardens at home.

7. they grow flowers in their yards.

8. plants can grow inside or outside.

9. a plant in a house needs water.

10. the sun helps plants grow.

11. did you ever see a garden in a jar?

12. you can learn how to grow one.

13. find a jar that is not too small.

14. put a little soil in the bottom.

15. then add some seeds.

Names of People

☞ Begin the first and last name of a person with a capital letter.

Darla Dancer went to the store.

☞ Begin titles of people with capital letters.

Mr. Bean owns the store.

☞ The word I is always written with a capital letter.

May I tell you something very silly?

✎ **Practice**

Read each sentence. Circle the letters that should be capital letters.

1. mike morton told me a story.

2. The story was about sandy simpson.

3. sandy bought a pound of shrimp.

4. jack jordan saw her put them on the floor.

5. brian black watched her, too.

6. Did alice acker go to the store?

7. mr. morton sold the shrimp.

8. Then ms. molly came in to buy bread.

9. Later dr. george walked into the store.

10. i don't believe what happened next.

11. i watched from the window.

12. i saw dr. george step on the shrimp!

Name _____ Date _____

Names of Places

☞ Begin the names of streets with capital letters.

I live on Williams Street.
My school is on Troy Avenue.

☞ Begin the names of cities and states with capital letters.

I live in Philadelphia.
It is a city in Pennsylvania.

✐ Practice

Read each sentence. Circle the letters that should be capital letters.

1. James Goss lives on peach street.

2. His friend Jerry lives on radish road.

3. James and Jerry walk to mushroom avenue.

4. They go to the store on strawberry road.

5. Next they will shop in the stores on pear place.

6. Tomorrow they plan to drive to marshmallow road.

7. James used to live in topeka.

8. It is in kansas.

9. James visited his sister in alaska.

10. She lives in the town of sitka.

11. James wants to visit new york.

12. Then he will go to texas.

Name _____ Date _____

Names of Days, Months, and Holidays

☞ Begin the name of a day of the week with a capital letter.

James Goss was sleepy on Wednesday.

☞ Begin the name of a month with a capital letter.

James' birthday is in January.

☞ Begin each important word in the name of a holiday with a capital letter.

James went to the fair on the Fourth of July.

✏ **Practice**

Read the sentences. Circle the letters that should be capital letters.

1. Betty Bean walked to work on monday.

2. She rode her bike on tuesday.

3. She visited on friday.

4. Tired Betty napped on sunday.

5. Betty Bean went sailing in april.

6. She went riding horses in august.

7. She made a snowball in december.

8. She flew a flag on flag day.

9. Betty celebrated thanksgiving with friends.

10. She had a party on labor day.

Name _____ Date _____

Titles of Books, Stories, and Poems

☞ Begin the first word, last word, and all important words in the title of a book with a capital letter. Draw a line under the title of a book.

<u>Journeys of Columbus</u>

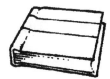

☞ Begin the first word, last word, and all important words in the title of a story or poem with a capital letter.

"Jonas and the Monster" (story)

"Something Is Out There" (poem)

✏ **Practice**

Read the sentences. Circle the letters that should be capital letters. Add underlines where they are needed.

1. I have a book called Columbus and the whale.

2. I also read a book called see my lovely flower garden.

3. A poem called "we bees" is in it.

4. Have you ever read the book called the dancing pony?

5. It has a poem called "an old story" in it.

6. I like the book the space child's poetry book.

7. I read the book where the rivers run.

Period (.)

☞ Use a **period** (.) at the end of a statement.

I like to read books about frogs.

☞ Put a period at the end of most titles of people.

Mr. Arnold Lobel wrote the book.

These are titles of people.

Mr.   **Mrs.**   **Ms.**

Dr.   **Miss**

✏ **Practice**

Correct the sentences. Add periods where they are needed.

1. John has a nice garden

2. The flowers are pretty

3. John gave Sara some seeds

4. Sara will plant them in the ground

5. Little green plants will grow

Correct the sentences. Add periods where they are needed.

6. Ms Sara thought the seeds were afraid.

7. Mr John told Sara not to worry.

8. Mrs Jones told Sara to wait a few days.

9. Sara showed her garden to Dr Dewey.

10. Ms Babbitt thinks Sara has a nice garden.

Name _____ Date _____

Question Mark (?), Exclamation Point (!), and Apostrophe (')

☞ Use a **question mark (?)** at the end of a question.

Who is Stewart?

☞ Use an **exclamation point (!)** at the end of an exclamation.

I don't care!

☞ Use an **apostrophe (')** to show that one or more letters have been left out in a contraction.

His parents didn't take Stewart anywhere.

✏ **Practice**

Finish the sentences correctly. Add question marks and exclamation points where they are needed.

1. Stewart just does not care

2. Would you rather stay here

3. Does Stewart care about anything

4. Yes, indeed he cares

Choose and circle the correct contractions.

5. Stewart said, "I (dont, don't) care!"

6. (Ill, I'll) get you," said the bear.

7. Stewart (didn't, didnt) want to stay with the bear.

Name _____ Date _____

Comma (,)

☞ Use a **comma (,)** between the name of a city and a state.

       Toledo, Ohio   **Albany, New York**

☞ Use a comma (,) between the day and the year in a date.

       July 4, 1776   **November 1, 1999**

☞ Use a comma (,) after the greeting and after the closing in a letter.

       Dear Mom and Dad,   **Your friend,**

 **Practice**

Read Mary Jane's letter to Grandmother. Put commas where they are needed.

January 8 1999

Dear Grandmother

   I hope you are feeling better. Yesterday Mom and I went shopping. We found a pretty new jacket for you. The tag says it comes from Chicago Illinois. I hope you like the jacket. Please write to me soon.

           Love
           Mary Jane

Name _____ Date _____

Unit Six Assessment: Kinds of Writing

Look at the picture. Choose one of the kinds of writing in the box. Circle your choice. Write about the picture using the kind of writing you choose. For example, if you choose <u>invitation</u>, you might write an invitation to someone to join you at the place shown in the picture.

story	rhyme	poem	friendly letter	invitation
thank-you note		journal	book report	

_____

_____

_____

_____

_____

_____

_____

_____

_____

Story

☞ In a **story** a writer tells about one main idea. Every story has a **beginning**, a **middle**, and an **ending**.

A Shadow Puppet Show

Last Saturday, Ken had a shadow puppet show at his house. First, he shut off the lights. Next, Ken shined a light on the wall. He moved his hands in the light. He made a shadow puppet duck on the wall! Everyone loved Ken's puppet show.

How to Write a Story

1. Write a beginning. Tell whom the story is about. Tell where the story takes place.
2. Write the middle. Tell what happens.
3. Write the ending. Tell how things work out.
4. Give the story a title. Underline the title.

 Practice

Finish the chart. Use the story above.

Beginning	Middle	Ending
1. Who is in the story? 2. Where does it happen?	3. What happens?	4. How do things work out?

Rhyme

☞ Words that end with the same sounds are **rhyming words**. Here are some rhyming words.

car-star   boat-goat   top-drop

☞ A **rhyme** is two or more lines that end with rhyming words. Many rhymes are silly or funny.

The cat took a rocket trip to the moon.

It left in July and came back in June.

How to Write a Rhyme

1. Write two lines.
2. End each line with a rhyming word.

✏ **Practice**

Finish each rhyme. Add rhyming words. You may use the words from the box.

cow	dog	bee	hat

1. Did you ever see a cat

Wear a funny _____?

2. The cat climbed down a tree

And sang a song with a _____.

3. The bee said, "meow,"

And flew away to visit the _____.

4. The cow watched a frog

Hop over a _____.

Unit Six: Kinds of Writing

Language Arts 2, SV 3888-3

Poem

☞ In a **poem** a writer paints a picture with words. Many poems have rhyming words at the end of every line or every other line.

Special Things

I like

White snow and blue bows.

I like

The sweet red rose.

I like

The crunchy sand between my toes.

I like

My puppy's wet black nose.

How to Write a Poem

1. End some lines with rhyming words.

2. Try to paint a picture with words.

3. Give your poem a title.

✎ **Practice**

Finish this poem. Think of describing words and words that rhyme. Give your poem a title.

_____

Summer is fun.

I can _____.

I feel so free

Like a _____.

Friendly Letter

☞ A **friendly letter** is a letter you write to someone you know.

☞ A friendly letter has five parts. They are the **heading**, **greeting**, **body**, **closing**, and **signature**.

August 10, 1999 ---------- **heading**

Dear Anne, ------------------------------- **greeting**

    I went to the zoo yesterday, and I saw
many animals. I like the lions best. What have --- **body**
you been doing? Write soon and tell me.

             Your friend, ------------ **closing**

             Pierre ------------------ **signature**

How to Write a Friendly Letter

1. Choose a friend or a relative to write to.
2. Write about things you have done.
3. Be sure your letter has five parts.
4. Use capital letters and commas correctly.

✎ Practice

Pretend Pierre is your friend. Think of three things you would tell him in a friendly letter. Write a letter to Pierre.

_____

_____

_____

_____

Invitation

☞ An **invitation** is a kind of letter. It asks someone to come somewhere.

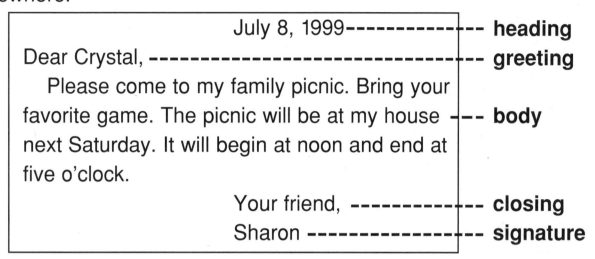

July 8, 1999 ------------------- **heading**

Dear Crystal, ------------------------------- **greeting**

    Please come to my family picnic. Bring your favorite game. The picnic will be at my house --- **body** next Saturday. It will begin at noon and end at five o'clock.

                    Your friend, ------------- **closing**
                    Sharon ------------------ **signature**

How to Write an Invitation

1. Tell who is invited and what the invitation is for.
2. Tell when to come and when to leave.
3. Tell where the events take place.
4. Use the five parts of a friendly letter.

✎ **Practice**

Write an invitation. Use the parts below.

1. October 1, 1999
2. Dear Amy,
3. Your friend,
4. Matthew
5. Please come to my party tomorrow. It will be at my house. It will begin at four o'clock. It will end at six o'clock.

_____

_____

_____

_____

_____

Name _____ Date _____

Thank-You Note

☞ A **thank-you note** is a short letter. It thanks someone for something he or she has given you or done for you.

> January 8, 1999 ----------- **heading**
> Dear Grandmother, ------------------------ **greeting**
> Thank you for the red coat you sent me. I wore it in the snow yesterday. It kept me ------- **body** warm and dry.
> Love, ------------------ **closing**
> Marti ------------------ **signature**

How to Write a Thank-You Note

1. Tell why you are thanking the person.
2. If you visited a place, tell why you enjoyed yourself.
3. If you were given a gift, say how you use it.
4. Use the five parts of a friendly letter.

✐ **Practice**

Write a thank-you note. Use the parts below.

1. June 27, 1999
2. Dear Aunt Penny,
3. Love,
4. Marti
5. Thank you for the sweater. It is very pretty. I will think of you when I wear it.

_____

_____

_____

_____

_____

Name _____ Date _____

Envelope

☞ An **envelope** is used to send a letter or a note.

Mary Jo Wood
13 West Street
Chicago, Illinois 60648 ---------------- return address

29¢ ---- stamp

Mrs. May Williams
13 River Bend Road ------------ mailing address
Crystal Lake, Illinois 60014

How to Address an Envelope

1. In the mailing address, tell who is receiving the letter.

2. In the return address, tell who is sending the letter.

3. Put a stamp on the envelope.

✏️ **Practice**

Use the envelope below. Address it to Mary Jo Wood. Use her address from the envelope above. Use your address as the return address.

Journal

☞   A writer uses a **journal** to tell about things that happen each day. You can use a journal to get ideas for your own writing.

April 5, 1999

Today Mom asked me to clean my closet. I found a lot of my old books and toys. I looked at the books and played with some of the toys. I found some pictures of me, too. I don't remember being so small!

How to Write a Journal

1. Write the date.
2. Write about something that happened that day.
3. Try to write something each day.

✎ **Practice**

Think about something that happened to you today. Write about it for your journal.

_____

_____

_____

_____

_____

Name _____ Date _____

Book Report

☞ A **book report** tells about a book. It also tells what you think about the book.

Title   The Koala
Author   Anita Best
About the Book   This book is about koalas. It tells many facts about this animal. Here are some of them. Koalas live in Australia. They live in trees. They eat leaves.
What I Think   This is a good book. I learned many things about koalas.

How to Write a Book Report

1. Write the title of the book. Underline it.

2. Write the author's name.

3. Tell some facts about the book.

4. Tell what you think about the book.

✏️ **Practice**

Answer these questions. Use the example book report above.

1. What is the title of the book?

_____

2. Who wrote the book?

_____

3. What did the writer of the report think about the book?

_____

Name _____ Date _____

Unit Seven Assessment: Paragraphs

✎ Look at the picture. Choose one of the kinds of paragraphs in the box. Circle your choice. Write a paragraph about the picture using the kind of paragraph writing you choose.

Note: Be sure to follow the rules for a good paragraph.
- Indent your first line.
- Write a sentence that tells the main idea.
- Write sentences that tell more about the main idea.

how-to paragraph (uses <u>first</u>, <u>next</u>, <u>then</u>, and <u>last</u>)
comparing paragraph (how things are alike)
contrasting paragraph (how things are different)
explaining paragraph (tells why things happen)
defining paragraph (tells what something means)
describing paragraph (uses describing words)
persuading paragraph (tells how you feel about something)

_____

_____

_____

_____

_____

_____

Paragraph

☞ A **paragraph** is a group of sentences that tell about one main idea. The first line of a paragraph is indented. This means the first word is moved in a little from the left margin.

☞ The first sentence in a paragraph often tells the main idea. The other sentences tell about the main idea.

> A safe home keeps people from getting hurt. Shoes or toys should not be left on the stairs. Matches, medicines, and cleaners should be locked safely away. Grown-ups should get things that are on high shelves for children. Then children will not fall and get hurt.

How to Write a Paragraph

1. Write a sentence that tells the main idea.
2. Indent the first line.
3. Write sentences that tell more about the main idea.

✐ **Practice**

Write three sentences that tell about this main idea.

There are many things you can do to be safe at school.

_____

_____

_____

_____

How-To Paragraph

☞ In a **how-to paragraph** a writer tells how to make or do something. The steps are told in order.

> Here is how to make a bird feeder. You will need a pine cone, string, peanut butter, and birdseed. First, tie the string to the top of the pine cone. Next, roll the pine cone in peanut butter. Then, roll the pine cone in birdseed. Last, go outside and tie the pine cone to a tree branch.

How to Write a How-To Paragraph

1. Write a sentence that tells what the paragraph is about.
2. Write a sentence that lists things you need.
3. Tell how to do something in order.
4. Use the words first, next, then, and last.

✏ Practice

Put these sentences for a how-to paragraph in order. Then write the paragraph. Remember to indent the first line.

1. Next, fill the can with water.
2. Last, water the plant.
3. Here is how to water a plant.
4. First, get a watering can.

_____

_____

_____

_____

Comparing Paragraph

☞ In a paragraph a writer can tell how two things are alike.

A killer whale and a dolphin are alike in how they look and where they live. A killer whale has smooth skin. It has a blowhole on top of its head. A dolphin also has a blowhole. The skin of a dolphin is smooth, too. A killer whale is a mammal that lives in the sea. A dolphin is also a sea mammal.

How to Write a Paragraph That Tells How Things Are Alike

1. Think of two things that are alike.
2. Write a sentence that tells how the two things are the same.
3. Add sentences that tell more about how the two things are alike.

✎ **Practice**

Write a comparing paragraph of your own. Follow the rules above.

_____

_____

_____

_____

_____

_____

_____

Name _____ Date _____

Contrasting Paragraph

☞ In a paragraph a writer can tell how two things are different.

Penguins and swallows are birds that live in different places. Penguins live where it is cold all year. They make their homes on the ground. Swallows live where it is warm. When winter comes they fly to find warm weather. Swallows build their nests in high places.

How to Write a Paragraph That Tells How Things Are Different

1. Think of two things that are different.
2. Write a sentence that tells how the two things are different.
3. Add sentences that tell more about how the two things are different.

✐ Practice

Write a contrasting paragraph of your own. Follow the rules above.

_____

_____

_____

_____

_____

_____

_____

Name _____   Date _____

Explaining Paragraph

☞ In a paragraph a writer can tell why something happens.

Mother was upset. She could not get the magic porridge pot to stop boiling. The pot would stop if she said the right words. Mother could not remember what words to say. So the pot kept boiling faster.

How to Write a Paragraph That Tells Why Something Happens

1. Write a sentence that tells what happens.
2. Add sentences that tell why it happens.
3. Write the sentences in order.

✐ **Practice**

Read each sentence that tells what happened. Then find the sentence in the next column that tells why it happened. Draw a line from the sentence that tells what happened to the sentence that says why it happened.

The little girl went looking
    for food.

There was so much porridge
    to eat.

The pot stopped boiling.

The little girl said the right words.

The people in the village
    were never hungry.

The little girl was hungry.

Language Arts 2, SV 3888-3

Name _____ Date _____

Defining Paragraph

☞ In a paragraph a writer can **define** a word. The writer tells what a word means.

> Love means something very special to me. It means spending special time with Grandfather. Love is holding Grandfather's big, warm hand. It is singing and laughing with him. Learning to fish with Grandfather is also love to me.

How to Write a Paragraph That Defines

1. Write a sentence that tells the word you are going to explain.
2. Add sentences that tell more about the word.
3. Use describing words and exact verbs in your sentences.

✐ **Practice**

Look at this drawing. Write words that define <u>happy</u> in the circles.

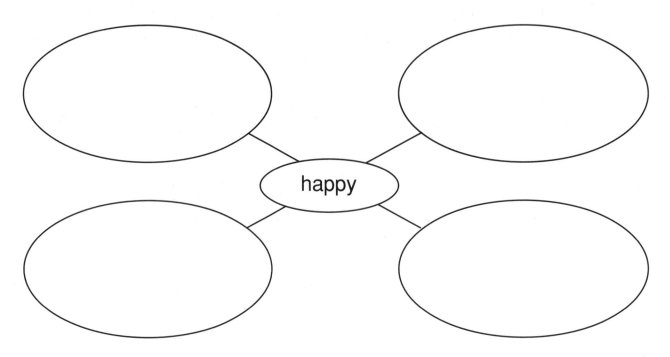

Name _____ Date _____

Describing Paragraph

☞ In a **paragraph that describes**, a writer tells about a person, place, or thing. The sentences have describing words that help the reader <u>see</u>, <u>hear</u>, <u>taste</u>, <u>smell</u>, and <u>feel</u>.

The little woman lived in a quiet little house. The house was painted brown and yellow. It had soft green grass around it. Huge orange and red flowers grew in a garden outside the house. The pretty flowers smelled sweet.

How to Write a Paragraph That Describes

1. Write a sentence that tells whom or what the paragraph is about.
2. Write sentences that tell more about the main idea.
3. Use describing words in your sentences.

✏ **Practice**

Finish the paragraph. Add describing words.

The little woman put on her _____ hat. She went

outside. It was a _____ day. The sky was

_____. The little woman felt _____.

Name _____ Date _____

Persuading Paragraph

☞ A paragraph can tell how a writer feels about something.

I think that a lizard should be our class pet. A lizard is small and easy to care for. It doesn't eat much food. Lizards are interesting to watch, too. Vote for the lizard!

How to Write a Paragraph That Tells How You Feel

1. Write about something you feel strongly about.
2. Tell how you feel in the first sentence.
3. Give reasons why other people should feel the same way.
4. Ask your reader to do something in the last sentence.

✏ **Practice**

Read this main idea. Then choose the sentences that best explain how the writer feels. Write the paragraph.

I think our family should get a dog.

1. Dogs make the best pets.
2. Dogs are friendly.
3. Cats are nice, too.
4. You can play lots of games with dogs.

_____

_____

_____

_____

Name _____ Date _____

About-You Paragraph

☞ A paragraph can tell about the writer.

One day my grandfather and I went to the zoo. First, we looked at lions and tigers. Next, we watched the monkeys play. Then, we went to see the bears. Last, Grandfather helped me feed the seals. My day with Grandfather was wonderful!

How to Write a Paragraph About Yourself

1. Write a sentence that tells about something that happened to you.
2. Write sentences that tell about what happened in order. Use the words first, next, then, and last.
3. Use the words I and me.

✎ **Practice**

Finish the paragraph. Add words that tell about yourself. Remember to indent the first line.

I had a good day at school. First, I _____

_____. Next, I _____

_____. Then, I ate lunch with my friend _____

_____. Last, I _____

_____.

Name _____ Date _____

Unit Eight Assessment: Book and Dictionary Skills

✏ Look at the example pages below. Answer the questions using the example pages. Tell if you used the <u>title page</u>, <u>table of contents</u>, or <u>index</u>.

<u>Flowers</u> <u>Everywhere</u> by Rose Peddle	**Contents** 1. Wildflowers . . . . 3 2. Greenhouses . . 9 3. Annuals. . . . . . 15 4. Bulbs. . . . . . . 20 5. Gardens 25	Annuals, 15-19 Bulbs, 20-25 Crocus, 22 Dandelions, 4, 8 Gardens, 6, 12, 17, 25-30 Zinnias, 17
title page	**table of contents**	**index**

1. What is the title of the book? _____

2. Who wrote the book? _____

3. How many chapters are in the book? _____

4. On what page does chapter 2 begin? _____

5. On what page would you find facts about dandelions? _____

✏ Look at the example dictionary page. Answer these questions.

253 tiny		total
ti•ny	[tī´nē] Very small.	
toad	[tōd] A small animal that is like a frog.	
to•day	[tə•dā´] This day.	
top•ic	[tŏ´pik] A subject in writing.	

6. What word would you find second on page 253? _____

7. Would you find the word <u>tune</u> on this page? _____

8. What entry word means "a subject in writing"? _____

9. What are the guide words on this page? _____

10. Could the word <u>toast</u> be on this page? _____

Unit Eight Assessment: Comprehension

✎ Read the story. Then answer the
questions about the story.

Night Visit

Elena, Michael, and their mother drove to Aunt Jean's house.
The children were the first to get out of the car. "Elena! Michael!"
Aunt Jean called from the house. The children ran to the house and
gave their aunt a big hug. Aunt Jean told the children about a doe
and a fawn that were in the woods behind the house.

"Maybe they will come see you while you are here," said
Aunt Jean.

That afternoon, the children looked out the window for the
deer. Nothing moved in the woods. It was very quiet. Aunt Jean
said she had left some food and water for them. She told the
children to be patient.

Elena could not fall asleep that night. The moon was shining
brightly into her room. When she got up to close the curtain, she
saw the doe and her fawn drinking the water. She ran to wake
everyone up.

1. How do the children feel about their aunt?_____

2. What does Aunt Jean have in her woods?_____

3. Why was Elena unable to fall asleep? _____

4. What happened after Elena got up to close the curtain? _____

_____

5. What do you think everyone will do next? _____

6. What is the main idea of the story? _____

Name _____ Date _____

Parts of a Book

☞ The **title page** tells the title of a book. It gives the name of the **author**. The author is the person who wrote the book.

☞ The **table of contents** lists the chapters or parts of the book. It tells the page where each chapter or part begins.

☞ Some books have an **index**. It is in ABC order. It tells the pages where things can be found.

Kinds of Houses	**Contents**	Apartments, 2, 7
by Jack Builder	1. Brick Houses 1	Basements, 25
	2. City Houses......5	Ceilings, 2, 9
	3. Country Houses..8	Concrete, 4, 16
	4. Wood Houses ..15	Doors, 12, 17
title page	**table of contents**	**index**

 **Practice**

Look at the example pages. Answer these questions. Tell if you used the <u>title page</u>, <u>table of contents</u>, or <u>index</u>.

1. What is the title of the book?

_____

2. Who wrote the book?

_____

3. How many chapters are in this book?

_____

4. On what page does chapter 4 begin?

_____

5. On which pages can you find facts about ceilings?

_____

Name _____   Date _____

Dictionary

☞ A **dictionary** is a book that lists words and their meanings. The words in a dictionary are listed in order from <u>A</u> to <u>Z</u>.

☞ The order of letters from <u>A</u> to <u>Z</u> is called **ABC order**. ABC order never changes.

a b c d e f g h i j k l m n o p q r s t u v w x y z

☞ Words can be put in ABC order. The first letters of these words were used to put them in ABC order.

<u>f</u>lower   <u>m</u>usic

<u>g</u>arden   <u>n</u>ight

<u>h</u>ome   <u>pl</u>ant

☞ Many words on a dictionary page begin with the same letter. When words begin with the same letter, the second letter is used to put the words in ABC order.

s<u>e</u>eds   g<u>a</u>rden

s<u>t</u>ory   g<u>r</u>een

s<u>u</u>n   g<u>u</u>ess

✏ **Practice**

Put each group of words in ABC order. Remember to use the <u>second</u> letter in each word if the first letter is the same.

1. noise _____   **3.** garden _____

music _____   ground _____

poem _____   frog _____

2. sun _____   **4.** afraid _____

rain _____   asleep _____

plant _____   alone _____

Name _____ Date _____

Dictionary

☞ The two words at the top of a dictionary page are called **guide words**. The word on the left is the first word on the page. The word on the right is the last word on the page. All the other words on the page are in ABC order between the first and the last word.

☞ An **entry word** is in **dark print** on a dictionary page. Entry words are in ABC order.

253
tiny   total

ti•ny   [tī′nē] Very small.
toad   [tōd] A small animal that is like a frog.
to•day   [tə•dā′] This day.
top•ic   [tŏp′ik] A subject in writing.

✏ Practice

Use the example dictionary page. Answer these questions.

1. Which word will you find first on page 253?

_____

2. Would you find the word <u>teeny</u> on this page?

_____

3. What entry word tells about an animal?

_____

4. What entry word means "very small"?

_____

5. Could the entry word <u>together</u> be on this page? Why or why not?

_____

Name _____ Date _____

Dictionary

☞ Some entry words have more than one meaning. Each meaning has a number.

☞ The dictionary has sentences that show how to use the entry word.

---

bump [bump] **1** To knock against: The goblin <u>bumped</u> against the tree. **2** A part that sticks out: The goblin fell over a <u>bump</u> in the road.

burst [burst] **1** To break apart suddenly: The balloon <u>burst</u>. **2** To give way to a strong feeling: Grandfather and I <u>burst</u> into laughter.

✐ **Practice**

Read the dictionary entries. Answer the questions.

1. What word can mean "to break apart"?

_____

2. What is the example sentence for meaning 2 of <u>burst</u>?

_____

3. Which word can mean "to knock against"?

_____

4. What is the number of the meaning of <u>bump</u> in this sentence?

The goblin fell over a <u>bump</u> in the road.

_____

5. Write your own example sentences for each meaning of <u>bump</u> and <u>burst</u>.

_____

_____

Kinds of Books

☞ Some books are called **fiction.** They are stories about make-believe people and things. Here are some titles of books that are fiction.

Ask Mr. Bear
The Bears Go to the Hospital

☞ **Nonfiction** books tell about real people or things. These books are nonfiction.

The Hospital Book
Who Keeps Us Safe?

☞ A library has fiction and nonfiction books. The fiction books are in one part of the library. The nonfiction books are in another part.

✏ **Practice**

Read about each book. Tell if the book is <u>fiction</u> or <u>nonfiction</u>.

1. a book about a magic bear

_____

2. a book that tells how to keep your home safe

_____

3. a book that tells how to ride a bicycle safely

_____

4. a book about a bear that can draw

_____

5. a book about a house that can talk

_____

6. a book about the fire department

_____

7. a book about a bear that is a nurse

_____

Drawing Conclusions

✐ Read the story. Think about the question as you read.

How do this husband and wife do the chores on their farm?

Foolish Farmers

Once upon a time, a husband and wife grew tired of living in the city. They decided to pack their things and move to a farm in the country. Since neither of them had ever lived on a farm, they asked a neighbor for help. The neighbor told them, "Milk the cow and plant the corn in the field."

So the wife poured some milk into a bucket and took it to the cow in the barn. She put the bucket of milk in front of the cow. "Drink the milk!" she cried to the cow. She patted the cow and was happy that she had milked the cow.

The husband woke up very early the next day to plant corn in the field. First, he found a bushel of corn-on-the-cob in the barn. "This will do nicely," he thought as he carried the bushel to the field. Then, he dug holes in the ground in even rows. Next, he took the ears of corn and planted them in the holes. He felt very proud of the work he had done.

The husband went back to the house. "Farm life is very easy," he said to his wife.

She agreed. "Yes. We should have left the city long ago."

Go on to the next page.

Name _____ Date _____

Drawing Conclusions

✎ Answer each question about the story. Circle the letter in front of the correct answer.

1. The neighbor probably knew _____.
   a. the husband and wife
   b. how to run a farm
   c. what the husband and wife would do
   d. all about the city

2. The cow most likely _____.
   a. still needs milking
   b. is happy with the milk
   c. belongs to the neighbor
   d. is lonely

3. The husband and wife think farm life is easy because _____.
   a. their chores were easy
   b. they have only one cow
   c. they only grow corn
   d. they do not do things correctly

4. You can tell that the husband and wife _____.
   a. are very smart
   b. know all about farming
   c. are not very clever
   d. have had a garden

Comparing and Contrasting

✐ Read the story. Think about the question as you read.

Why is Ollie different?

Ollie Ostrich

All the birds were very proud that they could fly. All the birds, that it, except Ollie. Ollie was an ostrich. She could not fly. She was not tiny like the other birds. Instead, she was large and fluffy and had long, strong legs. Ollie did not like being different from the other birds. Most of all, she wished that she could fly.

One day there was a terrible fire. Ollie and the other birds had to flee for their lives. As the fire grew, the smoke became so thick that the birds in the sky dropped to the ground. All, that is, except Ollie. She was already on the ground.

When she saw that the other birds were in trouble, she picked them up and put them on her big fluffy back. Then she ran as fast as she could with her long, strong legs. She carried the other birds to safety.

Afterwards, one of the little birds said to Ollie, "Thank you, Ollie. I wish I had long, strong legs like you." Ollie thought about that for a moment, and then she smiled a great big ostrich smile.

Go on to the next page.

Comparing and Contrasting

🖊 Answer each question about the story. Circle the letter in front of the correct answer.

1. What makes the other birds proud?
   a. Ollie can fly.
   b. They can fly.
   c. They can run.
   d. They are smart.

2. Which of these is NOT what makes Ollie different?
   a. Ollie is large and fluffy.
   b. Ollie has strong legs.
   c. Ollie is a bird.
   d. Ollie can run fast.

3. When the fire comes, what do the other birds do?
   a. They run away fast.
   b. They save Ollie.
   c. They hop away.
   d. They drop to the ground.

4. How does the little bird wish to be like Ollie?
   a. The little bird wants strong legs like Ollie.
   b. The little bird wants to fly like Ollie.
   c. The little bird likes Ollie's feathers.
   d. The little bird wants to be an ostrich.

Identifying Important Details

✏️ Read the story. Think about the question as you read.

What kind of pet does Mrs. Kelp get at the pet store?

Plenty of Pets

Mrs. Kelp wanted a pet to keep her company. She went to the pet store to look at the kittens and puppies. But when she got there, she saw a fat, fluffy white rabbit. Mrs. Kelp decided she would buy a rabbit.

When she got home she made a little bed for the rabbit, which she named Snowball. She played with Snowball and watched her hop around the house. Mrs. Kelp was very happy. A fluffy rabbit was the perfect pet.

One morning Mrs. Kelp went over to Snowball's little bed and found five baby rabbits nestled up to Snowball. Soon the baby rabbits grew up. Mrs. Kelp decided to give away some of the rabbits. She took the rabbits to the school near her house. She gave the rabbits to the teachers and the children. Everyone was very happy, and they thanked Mrs. Kelp very much for her gift.

When Mrs. Kelp went home, there were only two rabbits left. Snowball and one of her grown-up babies, named Snowshoe, were sound asleep in their bed.

Go on to the next page.

Identifying Important Details

 Answer each question about the story. Circle the letter in front of the correct answer.

1. Mrs. Kelp wanted a _____.
   a. friend
   b. pet
   c. house
   d. hat

2. She bought a _____.
   a. kitten
   b. puppy
   c. mouse
   d. rabbit

3. What did Snowball have?
   a. five babies
   b. five toys
   c. five sisters
   d. five teeth

4. How many rabbits did Mrs. Kelp keep?
   a. one
   b. two
   c. three
   d. four

Sequencing

✏ Read the story. Think about the question as you read.

What do Peter and his brother, Jimmy, do after school?

Best Brothers

Peter likes his big brother, Jimmy. Peter always waits for Jimmy to come home from school in the afternoon. He waves to Jimmy from the window, and this makes Jimmy smile. Peter always asks his big brother to play with him. Most of the time, Jimmy plays with his friends from school. Peter wishes that his big brother would play with him, too.

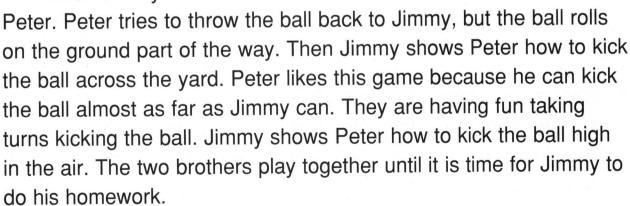

One day, Jimmy comes home from school and says, "Come on, Peter, let's go outside and play ball." Peter is so excited! They race to see who can get to the tree in the yard first. Jimmy wins.

Then Jimmy throws the ball to Peter. Peter tries to throw the ball back to Jimmy, but the ball rolls on the ground part of the way. Then Jimmy shows Peter how to kick the ball across the yard. Peter likes this game because he can kick the ball almost as far as Jimmy can. They are having fun taking turns kicking the ball. Jimmy shows Peter how to kick the ball high in the air. The two brothers play together until it is time for Jimmy to do his homework.

Go on to the next page.

Name _____   Date _____

Sequencing

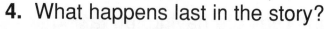 Answer each question about the story. Circle the letter in front of the correct answer.

1. When do Jimmy and Peter play together?
   a. when Peter gets home from the playground
   b. when Jimmy gets home from school
   c. before Jimmy goes to school
   d. after Jimmy does his homework

2. What happens first?
   a. Jimmy shows Peter how to kick the ball.
   b. Jimmy does his homework.
   c. Peter throws the ball to Jimmy.
   d. They race to the tree.

3. What do Peter and Jimmy do after they throw the ball?
   a. They kick the ball.
   b. They play checkers.
   c. They go to school.
   d. Jimmy comes home.

4. What happens last in the story?
   a. Peter and Jimmy throw the ball to each other.
   b. Peter and Jimmy kick the ball to each other.
   c. Jimmy shows Peter how to kick the ball high.
   d. Jimmy goes in to do his homework.

Identifying Cause and Effect

✏ Read the story. Think about the question as you read.

Why does the old man bring the dogs home?

So Many Dogs!

Once upon a time there was a nice old man and a nice old woman. They lived in a very pretty house that had flowers growing all around it. The old woman spent her time picking the flowers and putting them in every room in the house. Their house was always filled with beautiful flowers.

Something was wrong, though. The old man and the old woman were lonely. One day the old woman said to the old man, "I like taking care of my flowers, but I wish we had a dog."

So the man left his house and went to look for a dog. He walked by a farm. He saw a cow and a horse, but he did not see a dog. He walked into the forest. He saw a fox and a deer, but he did not see a dog. As he came out of the forest, he heard a funny sound. He looked across a field, and he knew what the sound was. It was the barking of dogs. The field was full of dogs! There were hundreds of dogs!

"I choose this dog," said the old man. Then he saw another dog that was so cute he could not bear to leave it behind. Before he knew it, he had chosen them all.

Go on to the next page.

Identifying Cause and Effect

✎   Answer each question about the story. Circle the letter in front of the correct answer.

1. The old man and the old woman are unhappy because _____.
   a. they cannot grow flowers
   b. they do not like their house
   c. they are lonely
   d. they have too many dogs

2. The old man left the house because _____.
   a. the old woman was angry
   b. he wanted to look for a dog
   c. he heard a funny sound
   d. he wanted to pick some flowers

3. The old man heard barking because _____.
   a. there was a dog in the house
   b. he saw a fox in the forest
   c. the field was full of dogs
   d. he wanted to find a dog

4. The old man chose all the dogs because _____.
   a. he did not like any of them
   b. they would not leave him alone
   c. the old woman wanted many dogs
   d. he could not bear to leave any behind

Making Judgments

✎ Read the story. Think about the question as you read.

How does Margaret's friend help?

A Good Friend

Margaret was sad because she could not go out to play. She watched her two brothers and their friends play outside. Margaret had broken her arm yesterday, and she was sad.

"Margaret, why don't you read a book?" her father asked.

"No, I don't feel like it." Margaret just sat and looked out the window. She played with her cat for a little while.

When the doorbell rang, Margaret thought that one of her brother's friends had come by. But instead, it was her friend Kim from school.

"Hello, Margaret," said Kim. "I heard you broke your arm."

"Yes, and I can't go outside to play," Margaret told her.

"Why don't we play in here?" Kim asked. "We could play a game or color some pictures." Margaret liked Kim's idea, and they played a game on the floor.

"I like playing this game with you," Margaret said. "Can you come to my house again tomorrow?"

Go on to the next page.

Making Judgments

✎   Answer each question about the story. Circle the letter in front of the correct answer.

1. Why did Margaret have to stay inside?
   a. She had no one to play with.
   b. Her brothers would not let her go out.
   c. She might hurt her arm again.
   d. It was too rainy outside.

2. Why did her father suggest reading a book?
   a. He was trying to help.
   b. He had too many books.
   c. He could not read.
   d. He wanted to go outside.

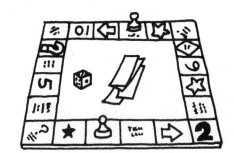

3. Kim came over because _____.
   a. she wanted to play outside
   b. she wanted to play with Margaret's brothers
   c. she knew Margaret could not go outside
   d. she had nothing else to do

4. Kim is a good friend because _____.
   a. she stays inside to play with Margaret
   b. she draws pictures with Margaret
   c. she goes to school with Margaret
   d. she knows that Margaret broke her arm

Summarizing

✎   Read each paragraph. Choose the answer that tells the most about the paragraph. Circle the letter in front of the correct answer.

1. Priscilla and Susan are friends, but they are not alike. Priscilla likes to read. She also likes to draw. Susan likes to run and jump. She likes to climb trees.

   a. Priscilla and Susan are different.

   b. Susan likes to climb trees.

   c. The two girls are friends, but Priscilla likes to stay quiet and Susan likes to keep moving.

   d. Priscilla and Susan are friends.

2. One day Susan was worried. She had to take a spelling test. She did not know how to study. Priscilla was a good speller. She said that she would help. The girls worked together. Susan did well on her test.

   a. Susan was worried about the spelling test.

   b. Priscilla helped Susan study and do well on her spelling test.

   c. Priscilla was a good speller.

   d. The girls worked together.

Go on to the next page.

Name _____   Date _____

Summarizing

✏ Read each paragraph. Choose the answer that
tells the most about the paragraph. Circle the letter in front of the
correct answer.

3. Peter sat in the woods. He was very quiet. He saw a rabbit hop
by. He saw two little chipmunks. Peter saw a squirrel. After a while,
he walked home. He was glad he had gone to the woods.

   a. Peter went to the woods.
   b. Peter saw two little chipmunks.
   c. Peter sat quietly in the woods and
       saw many animals.
   d. After a while, Peter walked home.

4. Josh and Selena like to play sports. They like to swim. They like
to play basketball. Once they went water-skiing. They want to try
many more sports.

   a. Josh and Selena like to play all kinds
       of sports.
   b. Josh and Selena went water-skiing.
   c. Josh and Selena play basketball.
   d. They want to try many more sports.

Name _____ Date _____

Predicting Outcomes

🖊 Read each paragraph. Choose the answer that tells what will probably happen next. Circle the letter in front of the correct answer.

1. Carlos walked to the dock. The dock had a rotten board. Carlos did not see the board. Then Carlos stepped onto the rotten board.

   a. Carlos will take his foot off the board.
   b. Someone will tell Carlos about the board.
   c. Carlos will put his foot through the board.
   d. Someone will fix the rotten board.

2. Jill heard the music of the ice cream truck. She raced to find her father. Jill's father gave her some money. Jill ran out the front door. She saw the ice cream truck parked down the street.

   a. Jill will buy an ice cream cone from
      the truck.
   b. The ice cream truck will turn around.
   c. Jill's father will take back the money.
   d. Jill will buy a hot dog from the truck.

Go on to the next page.

Predicting Outcomes

✏ Read each paragraph. Choose the answer that tells what will probably happen next. Circle the letter in front of the correct answer.

3. Brad found his fishing rod. Then he got his bike. He went to his friend's house. His friend had his fishing rod, too. They rode their bikes to the river.

- **a.** Brad and his friend will go boating.
- **b.** Brad will ride back to his house.
- **c.** Brad's friends will get a new bike.
- **d.** The boys will go fishing in the river.

4. Tina puts some bread in a bag. She walks to the lake. There are ducks swimming in the lake.

- **a.** Tina will run away from the ducks.
- **b.** Tina will feed the ducks some bread.
- **c.** Tina will eat bread.
- **d.** Tina will talk to the ducks.

Name _____ Date _____

Identifying the Main Idea

✎ Read each paragraph. Choose the answer that tells the main idea of the paragraph. Circle the letter in front of the correct answer.

Toys have been around for many years. The earliest toys were very simple. There were dolls and animal toys. They had no moving parts. Toys made today can have many moving parts. They are very different from the toys of the past!

1. Which of these tells the main idea of the paragraph?

   a. Toys made today can have many moving parts.
   b. There were dolls and animal toys.
   c. Toys have been around for many years.
   d. They had no moving parts.

I love to go sliding in the snow. I like to skate on the ice. I like taking walks on snowy nights. I especially like sitting by a warm fire and reading a book on a winter evening. Winter is my favorite season of the year.

2. Which of these tells the main idea of the paragraph?
   a. I love to go sliding in the snow.
   b. Winter is my favorite season of the year.
   c. I like to skate on the ice.
   d. I like taking walks on snowy nights.

Go on to the next page.

Name _____   Date _____

Identifying the Main Idea

✏️ Read each paragraph. Choose the answer that tells the main idea of the paragraph. Circle the letter in front of the correct answer.

Terry is five years old. He thinks he is old enough to walk to school by himself. His mother is not so sure. She wants him to wait until he is six. Terry tries to remember all the safety rules. Every morning, he asks his mother whether he can walk to school by himself.

3. Which of these tells the main idea of the paragraph?
   a. Terry tries to remember all the safety rules.
   b. Terry is five years old.
   c. She wants him to wait until he is six.
   d. He thinks he is old enough to walk to school by himself.

Darcy has many pets. She has two dogs, five cats, and three rabbits. Every time Darcy finds an animal that is hurt or lost, she takes it home with her. If she cannot find the owner, Darcy's parents let her keep the animals as long as she takes care of them.

4. Which of these tells the main idea of the paragraph?
   a. Darcy has many pets.
   b. She has two dogs, five cats, and three rabbits.
   c. If she cannot find the owners, Darcy's parents let her keep the animals.
   d. Every time Darcy finds an animal that is hurt or lost, she takes it home with her.

Name _____ Date _____

Distinguishing Between Reality and Fantasy

 Read the story. Think about the question as you read.

Which parts of this story could really happen?

Sasha Spider

Sasha watched as the other spiders crawled up the walls of the barn and spun beautiful webs in the corners by the ceiling.

"I wish I could spin a web up there," said Sasha. But she was afraid of high places. Every time she tried to climb, she got dizzy and fell.

One day, a boy entered the barn. He almost stepped on Sasha's web!

"Look out!" cried Sasha to the boy.

"Oh! I'm sorry," said the boy. "Let me help you. I'll lift you up high so that you can build a web in a safe place."

Before she knew it, Sasha was high up on the barn wall. She was too afraid to come back down, so she made a web! The other spiders came over and admired it. All the spiders remarked on how beautiful Sasha's web was. Sasha forgot about being afraid. After that, she always found a high place in the barn for her web.

Go on to the next page.

Name _____ Date _____

Distinguishing Between Reality and Fantasy

✏ Answer each question about the story. Answer <u>YES</u> if what happens in the sentence could really happen. Answer <u>NO</u> if what happens in the sentence could not really happen.

1. Sasha watched as the other spiders crawled up the walls of the barn and spun beautiful webs in the corners by the ceiling. _____

2. "I wish I could spin a web up there," said Sasha. _____

3. One day, a boy entered the barn. _____

4. He almost stepped on Sasha's web! _____

5. "Look out!" cried Sasha to the boy. _____

6. All the spiders remarked on how beautiful Sasha's web was. ___

Understanding Problems and Solutions

Read the story. Think about the question as you read.

What is the old man's problem?

The Old Man and the Cow

Once upon a time, long, long ago, a little old man lived in a small cottage near the forest. The little old man was very gentle and kind. Every morning he woke up and sang a merry tune as he fed his chickens and milked his cow. Then he would take the milk to the village to trade for cheese, fruit, and fresh bread.

One morning, much to the little old man's surprise, his cow was gone! He looked for his cow in the garden. He looked in the woods. The cow was nowhere to be found. So the little old man went to search for it.

He walked and walked until he was quite tired. When he was almost to the village, he saw his cow running and playing with the other cows in a big, grassy field. His cow looked so happy! But the little old man called to his cow and took her back home.

He thought nothing more of it until the same thing happened the next day and the next. Each morning, when he went to milk his cow, she was gone. Each morning, the little old man would  walk to the big, grassy field and take his cow home. The little old man did not know what to do.

Go on to the next page.

Name _____ Date _____

Understanding Problems and Solutions

✏ Answer each question about the story.

1. What does the old man want to do?

_____

2. What does the cow want to do?

_____

3. What is the problem?

_____

4. What could the old man do to solve his problem?

_____

5. Write your own ending to the story and tell how the problem
   is solved.

_____

_____

_____

_____

Language Arts Handbook
Grade Two
Answer Key

P. 5   Unit One Assessment: 1. king, cup, 2. home, who, 3. scene, ceiling, 4. jar, gym, 5. come, kick, 6. nice, gnat, 7. write, rice, 8. knock, nice, 9.-28. Some letters may work with more than one ending; most likely answers: 9. true, 10. frog, 11. crayon, 12. green, 13. brother, 14. speck, 15. snap, 16. smell, 17. skirt, 18. stay, 19. split, 20. spring, 21. shrunk, 22. strong, 23. throat, 24. chunk, 25. twice, 26. phone, 27. sheep, 28. them

P. 6   Unit One Assessment: 1. shell, doll, 2. cliff, muff, 3. page, bridge, 4. voice, class, 5. is, fuzz, 6. black, look, 7. glass, rice, 8. cottage, village, 9.-28. Some letters may work with more than one beginning; most likely answers: 9. first, 10. squint, 11. world, 12. round, 13. task, 14. each, 15. brush, 16. grasp, 17. gift, 18. teeth, 19. spring, 20. burst, 21. drink, 22. laugh, 23. graph, 24. sound, 25. desk, 26. dish, 27. fling, 28. soft

P. 7   Unit One Assessment: 1. would, good, 2. base, snail, 3. play, tail, 4. key, leaf, 5. pity, field, 6. see, me, 7. ride, bright, 8. kind, sky, 9. pie, high, 10. open, goat, 11. blow, road, 12. rope, old, 13. use, fuse, 14. dune, tube, 15. two, boot, 16. chew, soup, 17. horn, warm, 18. door, more, 19. heard, serve, 20. girl, word, 21. turn, her, 22. farm, yarn, 23. care, chair, 24. bear, hair, 25. cheer, dear

P. 8   1. tell, too, 2. pin, poor, 3. my, man, 4. gone, gold

P. 9   1. boat, 2. week, 3. now, 4. fox, 5. worm, 6. young, 7. lion, 8. zoo, 9. duck, 10. vase, 11. yard, 12. van

P. 10   1. giraffe, joke, giant, just, job, gym, 2. said, cent, soon, scent, city, sausage

P. 11   1. king, cup, 2. home, who, 3. hat, house, 4. cow, kitten, 5. kite, cave, 6. cold, cat, 7. carrot, keep, 8. happy, hut, 9. come, kick, 10. hit, horse, 11. key, kind, 12. hello, help, 13. cage, cane, 14. kite, cut, 15. whom, hen

P. 12   1. neat, knew, none, gnaw, gnat, know, 2. ring, wrong, ruler, wrap, robin, wrote

P. 13   1. brother, 2. green, 3. frog, 4. fresh, 5. crack, 6. broken, 7. true, 8. ground, 9. crayon, 10. from, 11. cream, 12. treat

P. 14   1. sky, skip, 2. stay, step, stamp, stop, 3. smart, smoke, smell, 4. spoke, sport, speck, 5. snake, snap, snout

P. 15   1. splash, 2. spray, 3. squirrel, 4. shrink, 5. street, 6. squint, 7. squeeze, 8. shrunk, 9. spring, 10. squeak, 11. strong, 12. splinter

P. 16   1. twins, twinkle, twig, twice, twelve, 2. throne, throat, through, throw, thread

P. 17   1. shark, 2. chicken, 3. then, 4. cheese, 5. shirt, 6. they, 7. them, 8. ship, 9. the, 10. sheep, 11. phonograph, 12. phone

P. 18   1. muff, 2. ball, 3. cliff, 4. doll, 5. cuff, 6. shell, 7. mill, 8. hill, 9. well

P. 19   1. page, bridge, 2. voice, class, 3. is, fuzz, 4. whiz, has, 5. clock, book, 6. has, fuzz, 7. cottage, village, 8. black, cook

P. 20   1. lift, 2. squint, 3. world, 4. friend, 5. around, 6. clasp, 7. mask, 8. gift, 9. grasp, 10. past, 11. want, 12. kind, 13. test, 14. gold, 15. ask

P. 21   1. bank, 2. rang, 3. thing, 4. brush, 5. wish, 6. rough, 7. mouth, 8. thank, 9. photograph, 10. bunk, 11. much, 12. teeth, 13. such, 14. skunk, 15. drink, 16. dish, 17. each, 18. laugh, 19. which, 20. hunting

P. 22   1. plan, back, 2. touch, rug, 3. pot, mop, 4. win, is, 5. bread, red

P. 23   1. hood, 2. would, 3. cook, 4. foot, 5. good, 6. could, 7. stood, 8. brook, 9. look, 10. shook, 11. brook, 12. foot, 13. good, 14. hood, 15. cook

P. 24   1. name, 2. late, 3. way, 4. take, 5. day, 6. rain, 7. same, 8. came, 9. stay, 10. lake, 11. date, 12. snail

P. 25   1. key, 2. seed, 3. pea, 4. chief, 5. carry, 6. she, 7. we, 8. field, 9. teeth, 10. happy, 11. turkey, 12. reach

P. 26   1. fly, 2. tie, 3. right, 4. find, 5. cry, 6. why, 7. might, 8. side, 9. high, 10. bike, 11. time, 12. fright, 13. try, 14. bright, 15. like

P. 27   1. boat, 2. home, 3. oh, 4. snow, 5. go, 6. blow, 7. old, 8. bone, 9. toad, 10. nose, 11. low, 12. troll, 13. so, 14. bowl, 15. coat, 16. grow, 17. cold, 18. road

P. 28   1. tune, 2. cube, 3. fuse, 4. excuse, 5. tube, 6. dune, 7. huge

P. 29   1. goose, 2. who, 3. tool, 4. group, 5. chew, 6. zoo, 7. moon, 8. room

P. 30   1. shore, 2. torn, 3. store, 4. sport, 5. floor, 6. corn, 7. horse, 8. warn, 9. more, 10. north

P. 31   1. bird, 2. earth, 3. serve, 4. world, 5. hurt, 6. first, 7. skirt, 8. burn, 9. work, 10. learn, 11. bird, 12. burn, 13. skirt, 14. learn

P. 32   1. fair, wear, care, hair, dare, pear, 2. steer, clear, near, 3. hard, cart, dark

P. 33   1. winter, 2. sweater, 3. river, 4. motor, 5. father, 6. dollar, 7. supper, 8. feather, 9. flower, 10. color

P. 34   1. joy, coin, point, choice, toy, 2. loud, out, pound, how, town

P. 35   Unit Two Assessment: 1. adjective, 2. verb, 3. noun, 4. pronoun, 5. contraction, 6. verb, 7. noun, 8. compound word, 9. pronoun, 10. contraction, 11. verb, 12. verb, 13. adjective, 14. compound word, 15. adjective

P. 36   1. house, thing, 2. ceiling, thing, 3. closet, thing, 4. hat, thing, 5. shoe, thing, 6. boy, person 7.-12. Answers may vary; possible answers: 7. girl, 8. store, 9. song, 10. floor, 11. man, 12. woman

P. 37   1. Where did Jack Sprat go?, 2. Mary saw her friend Jill., 3. Did Mr. or Mrs. Sprat go with them?, 4. They met Ms. Muffet along the way., 5. They walked along Michigan Avenue., 6. Then they drove through Indiana and Ohio.

P. 38   1. Wednesday, 2. February, 3. Saturday, 4. July, 5. Thanksgiving

P. 39   1. boys, 2. girl, 3. robe, 4. stars, 5. moon, 6. house, 7. door, 8. treats, 9. cats, 10. dogs, 11. owl, 12. stars, 13. trees, 14. hands, 15. song

P. 40   A. Answers may vary. 1. travel, 2. drive, 3. visit, 4. ride, 5. climb, 6. take, 7. run, 8. jog, 9. fly, 10. zoom B. Stories will vary.

P. 41   1. skips, 2. play, 3. hug, 4. purrs, 5. barks, 6. hide, 7. waves, 8. blows, 9. follows, 10. sees, 11. jumps, 12. hears, 13. move, 14. hoots, 15. take, 16. eat, 17. chews, 18. begs

P. 42   A. 1. plays, 2. runs, 3. dance, 4. wait, 5. leaps, B. takes, sits, asks, takes, walks, hits

P. 43   1. played, 2. visited, 3. looked, 4. jumped, 5. leaned, 6. walked, 7. laughed, 8. wanted, 9. opened, 10. poured, 11. walked, 12. helped

P. 44   1. are, 2. are, 3. were, 4. is, 5. are, 6. were, 7. is, 8. am, 9. was, 10. is

P. 45   1. has, 2. have, 3. had, 4. has, 5. have, 6. have, 7. has, 8. have, 9. has, 10 have

P. 46   1. ran, 2. came, 3. went, 4. go, 5. run, 6. goes, 7. went, 8. came, 9. came, 10. ran

P. 47   Answers may vary. 1. pink, 2. long, 3. Brown, 4. round, 5. juicy, 6. tiny

P. 48   1. tired, 2. happy, 3. many, 4. one, 5. hungry, 6. some, 7. three, 8. sleepy

P. 49   2. brighter, 3. tallest, 4. fast, 5. thicker, 6. biggest, 7. wider, 8. oldest

P. 50   1. We, 2. S/he, 3. S/he, 4. It. 5. S/he, 6. It. 7. They, 8. We, 9. They, 10. We

P. 51   1. sunglasses, 2. afternoon, 3. playground, 4. birthday, 5. outside, 6. scrapbook, 7. sunglasses, 8. playground, 9. outside, 10. afternoon, 11. scrapbook, 12. birthday

P. 52   1. isn't, 2. can't, 3. hadn't, 4. wasn't, 5. haven't, 6. didn't, 7. don't, 8. hasn't

P. 53   Unit Three Assessment: 1. Bear, 2. tree, 3. ride, 4. ran, 5. grow, 6. mailed, 7. statement, 8. asking, 9. exclamation, 10. I planted and watered the seeds. 11. The flowers grew and were pretty. 12. Sentences will vary; e.g. The long train raced by me on the tracks.

P. 54   Answers will vary.

P. 55   1. statement, 2. question, 3. statement, 4. question, 5. statement, 6. question, 7. exclamation, 8. statement, 9. question, 10. exclamation

P. 56   1. John gave seeds to Sara and told her to plant them., 2. Sara planted the seeds and looked at the ground., 3. Sara sang songs and read stories to her seeds. 4. The rain fell on the seeds and helped them grow.

P. 57   1. The farmer and his family stood in the doorway., 2. The hunter and the bear stayed with the family., 3. The mice and the children ran out the door., 4. The hunter and the bear went home.

    Language Arts 2, SV 3888-3

P. 58   Answers will vary. Examples: 1. Sam is a little moth., 2. Can Sam feel the cool breeze?, 3. The pond was Sam's favorite place., 4. The children put Sam in a glass jar., 5. Sam flew back to the little pond.

P. 59   1. The ant climbed down a blade of grass. S/he fell into the spring., 2. The bird pulled off a leaf. H/She let it fall into the water., 3. The hunter saw a lion. S/He spread his net., 4. The lion and I live in the woods. We are friends.

P. 60   Answers will vary. Examples: 1. stroll, 2. race, 3. peddle, 4. speed, 5. zooms, 6. jogs, 7. skip, 8. travels

P. 61   Unit Four Assessment: 1. house, 2. tune, 3. wonderful, 4. close, 5. found, 6. worst, 7. un, 8. ly, 9. mis, 10. less, 11. able, 12. re, 13. too, 14. their, 15. me, 16. two, 17. there

P. 62   1. home, 2. couch, 3. seat, 4. plates, 5. pal, 6. cap, 7. carpet, 8. song

P. 63   1. new, old, 2. down, up, 3. day, night, 4. tall, short, 5. big, little, 6. late, 7. down, 8. close, 9. walk, 10. dry, 11. cool, 12. sunny

P. 64   1. unable; not able, 2. reopened; opened again, 3. unlucky; not lucky; 4. unfair; not fair, 5. unhappy; not happy, 6. rewind; wind again, 7. rewashed; washed again, 8. uneven; not even, 9. refilled; filled again, 10. reknitted; knitted again

P. 65   1. cheerful; full of cheer, 2. careful; full of care, 3. harmless; without harm, 4. breakable; able to be broken, 5. useless; without use, 6. dreadful; full of dread, 7. hopeful; full of hope, 8. thankful; full of thanks

P. 66   1. two, 2. too, 3. to, 4. too, 5. to, 6. two, 7. two, 8. too, 9. to, 10. too, 11. two, 12. to, 13. too, 14. to, 15. two

P. 67   1. their, 2. They're, 3. there, 4. their, 5. there, 6. They're, 7. They're, 8. there, 9. there, 10. Their, 11. there, 12. They're

P. 68   1. I, 2. me, 3. me, 4. I, 5. Susan and I, 6. Tina and me, 7. Tina and I, 8. Susan and me

P. 69   Unit Five Assessment: 1. My Uncle John likes to have a garden., 2. He lives on Smith Street., 3. Can you come with me on Tuesday, June 3?, 4. I am reading a book called Great Gardens., 5. It has pictures of giant plants!, 6. Mr. Lopez lives near my uncle. 7. Don't you think it would be nice to visit him?, 8. In August, the garden will have many vegetables.

P. 70   1-15: The first letter in each sentence should be circled.

P. 71   Listed are the words that should be capitalized: 1. Mike Morton, 2. Sandy Simpson, 3. Sandy, 4. Jack Jordan, 5. Brian Black, 6. Alice Acker, 7. Mr. Morton, 8. Ms. Molly, 9. Dr. George, 10. I, 11. I, 12. I, Dr. George

P. 72   Listed are the words that should be capitalized: 1. Peach Street, 2. Radish Road, 3. Mushroom Avenue, 4. Strawberry Road, 5. Pear Place, 6. Marshmallow Road, 7. Topeka, 8. Kansas, 9. Alaska, 10. Sitka, 11. New York, 12. Texas

P. 73   Listed are the words that should be capitalized. 1. Monday, 2. Tuesday, 3. Friday, 4. Sunday, 5. April, 6. August, 7. December, 8. Flag Day, 9. Thanksgiving, 10. Labor Day

P. 74   1. I have a book called Columbus and the Whale., 2. I also read a book called See My Lovely Flower Garden., 3. A poem called "We Bees" is in it., 4. Have you ever read the book called The Dancing Pony?, 5. It has a poem called "An Old Story" in it., 6. I like the book The Space Child's Poetry Book., 7. I read the book Where the Rivers Run.

P. 75   1-5; each sentence should end with a period., 6. Ms., 7. Mr., 8. Mrs., 9. Dr., 10., Ms.

P. 76   1. !, 2. ?, 3. ?, 4. !, 5. don't, 6. I'll, 7. didn't

P. 77   January 8, 1999/ Dear Grandmother,/ I hope you are feeling better./ Yesterday Mom and I went shopping./ We found a pretty new jacket for you. /The tag says it comes from Chicago, Illinois./ I hope you like the jacket./ Please write to me soon./ Love, Mary Jane

P. 78   Unit Six Assessment: Answers will vary. Writing should relate to the picture and follow the form that the student chooses.

P. 79   1. Ken, some people at his house, 2. It happens at his house., 3. First, Ken shut off the lights. Next, he shined a light on the wall. Then he moved his hands in the light. He made a puppet duck on the wall., 4. Everyone loved Ken's puppet show.

P. 80   Answers may vary, but must rhyme. 1. hat, 2. bee, 3. cow, 4. dog

P. 81   Poems will vary, but should use rhyming describing words and have a title.

P. 82   Letters will vary, but should have the elements of the letter-

P. 83   heading, greeting, body, closing, signature.

P. 83   Invitation using the provided information.

P. 84   Thank-you note using the provided information.

P. 85   Addressed envelope using Mary Jo Wood as addressee and student's name and address in return address area.

P. 86   Journal entries will vary; should include date.

P. 87   1. The Koala, 2. Anita Best, 3. The writer thought this was a good book. The writer learned many things about koalas.

P. 88   Unit Seven Assessment: Paragraphs will vary but should relate to the picture. First line should be indented; student should include a sentence with the main idea and some sentences to support the main idea. The paragraph should be the type the student chose to write.

P. 89   Answers will vary. Sentences should be about school safety.

P. 90   1. Here is how to water a plant., 2. First, get a watering can., 3. Next, fill the can with water., 4. Last, water the plant.

P. 91   Paragraphs will vary, but should compare two things, have a sentence with the main idea, and supporting sentences.

P. 92   Paragraphs will vary, but should contrast two things, have a sentence with the main idea, and supporting sentences.

P. 93   Line from The little girl went looking for food. to The little girl was hungry.; Line from The pot stopped boiling. to The little girl said the right words.; Line from The people in the village were never hungry. to There was so much porridge to eat.

P. 94   Students write words that define happy in the circles; examples; ice cream, my family, riding my bike, etc.

P. 95   Students' describing words will vary; examples: The little woman put on her best hat. She went outside. It was a sunny day. The sky was blue. The little woman felt happy.

P. 96   Students write a paragraph using the sentences except sentence 3, which does not relate to the paragraph.

P. 97   Students choice of words will vary; examples: I had a good day at school. First, I read a book. Next, I did math. Then, I ate lunch with my friend Jack. Last, I painted a picture.

P. 98   Unit Eight Assessment: 1. Flowers Everywhere; title page, 2. Rose Peddle; title page, 3. 5; table of contents, 4. 9; table of contents, 5. 4, 8; index, 6. toad, 7. no, 8. topic, 9. tiny, total, 10. yes

P. 99   1. They love her., 2. a doe and a fawn, 3. The moon was too bright., 4. She saw the doe and fawn., 5. They will look at the deer., 6. The children get to see the doe and fawn that are in Aunt Jean's backyard.

P. 100   1. Kinds of Houses; title page, 2. Jack Builder; title page, 3. 4; table of contents, 4. 15; table of contents, 5. 2, 9; index

P. 101   1. music, noise, poem, 2. plant, rain, sun, 3. frog, garden, ground, 4. afraid, alone, asleep

P. 102   1. tiny, 2. no, because teeny comes before tiny in the alphabet, and tiny is the first word on this page, 3. toad, 4. tiny, 5. yes, because the word together falls between tiny and total in ABC order.

P. 103   1. burst, 2. Grandfather and I burst into laughter., 3. bump, 4. 2, 5. Answers will vary; examples: I have a bump on my head., The water pipe burst.

P. 104   1. fiction, 2. nonfiction, 3. nonfiction, 4. fiction, 5. fiction, 6. nonfiction, 7. fiction

P. 106   1. b, 2. a, 3. d, 4. c

P. 108   1. b, 2. c, 3. d, 4. a

P. 110   1. b, 2. d, 3. a, 4. b

P. 112   1. b, 2. d, 3. a, 4. d

P. 114   1. c, 2. b, 3. c, 4. d

P. 116   1. c, 2. a, 3. c, 4. a

P. 117   1. c, 2. b

P. 118   3. c, 4. a

P. 119   1. c, 2. a

P. 120   3. d, 4. b

P. 121   1. c, 2. b

P. 122   3. d, 4. a

P. 124   1. yes, 2. no, 3. yes, 4. yes, 5. no, 6. no

P. 126   1. He wants to milk his cow., 2. The cow wants to play., 3. The old man cannot milk the cow if she is gone off to play, and then he cannot sell the milk in town., 4. Answers will vary; possibly the cow and old man could agree that the cow could play after milking. 5. Story endings will vary, should try to solve the problem.

   Language Arts 2, SV 3888-3